COMFORT IN
THE CHAOS

Deep Thoughts on God and Faith

Dr. Doug Corrigan

Doug Corrigan
Please visit www.ScienceWithDrDoug.com

Printed in the United States of America

First Printing: September 2020

ISBN- 9798768109851

"Are not two sparrows sold for a penny? Yet not one of them will fall to the ground outside your Father's care. And even the very hairs of your head are all numbered. So don't be afraid; you are worth more than many sparrows" - Matthew 10:29-31.

—JESUS

About the Author

Doug grew up in New Jersey and became a Christian in his mid-teen years. Being a scientist, he enjoys exploring deeper thoughts covering faith, philosophy, and science. He is the author of the book, "The Author of Light," which explores how God designed the laws of nature in such a way that they would tell a story about who He is.

Doug is married to Amy and is father to three daughters and one son. In his spare time, Doug enjoys composing piano music.

You can contact Doug for speaking engagements or with any questions by emailing:
DrDougCorrigan@gmail.com

You can find more content developed by Dr. Doug Corrigan at:
www.ScienceWithDrDoug.com

Acknowledgements

I would like to thank God for always being there for me, especially during the times I didn't know He was.

CONTENTS

PREFACE

I think it would be an understatement to say that these last two years have been a bit stressful for most of us. Many of us have found ourselves losing loved ones, being afraid that we are going to become sick and die, being concerned about tough decisions, losing our job, and generally uncertain about the hopelessness that seems to define our immediate future. Have you felt this way? Does it feel like the entire world started spinning out of control? Have you found yourself wondering, "will things every get back to 'normal'?"

It's in times like these that our faith and our relationship with God are tested. I must be honest here – I've found my faith tested through this increasingly tumultuous time. But I've also found myself relying more and more on God – more than any other time in my life. When the world we knew starts falling out from under our feet, we look up. And that's a good thing.

Anxiety, worry, and fear are all cousins. But these aren't the kind of cousins you want visiting or coming around to the family reunion. I've found that most of our problems stem from this trinity of vexation, not the actual problems we find ourselves fantasizing about. I don't mean to minimize real loss that any of us have experienced, but I think more often than not our feelings of coming undone are related to our perception of reality, rather than reality itself.

This becomes increasingly apparent when we decide to exit this world and enter into another, even for a brief time. When we pause for a moment and read a passage of God's Word, or we have a conversation with God, we immediately feel the worry, anxiety, and fear dissipate. We know this to be the case, but many of us resist spending time with God or digging into His Word. Many of us know what we need to do, but we don't. Human nature, for some reason, wants us to remain miserable. I believe that this current period of turmoil time has made many of us realize in a very real way that our flesh is at war with our spirit.

Leading up to this time, and through this time, I have written short devotions that I have shared on social media. These short articles are meant to help remind you to reconnect with God, explore faith at a deeper level, or to help you see things from a different perspective.

I've collected these articles and edited them to compose this book. My hope is that this book of devotions serves as a source to spur you on to go deeper in your relationship with God and to remain grounded in your faith, even as the world continues to decay around us.

Our hope is not found in our circumstances; our hope is found in Christ. Everything else will eventually disappear, but Jesus will remain. Therefore, we ought to attach our thoughts, hopes, and faith to Christ.

I pray that this book will serve as a constant source of hope, joy, peace, and reflection in your life, and those of your loved ones.

What If?

I think the current crisis has taught our brains to constantly ask, "what if?"

What if I get sick?
What if my parents get sick?
What if my kids get sick?

And this leads to other 'what ifs?'

What if I lose my job?
What if I lose my house?

Our brains quickly become adapted to dwelling on this question. It permeates the way we think, and becomes a habit that shapes the way we see the world. Our brains become addicted to this cycle of negative reinforcement and fear, and it quickly becomes the filter by which we see the entire world.

We run through all of the worst-case scenarios in our imagination, and we feel all of the stress, fear, anxiety, and helplessness as we're imagining these hypothetical scenarios, just as if we had actually experienced the traumatic event we're worrying about. Our pulse goes up, adrenaline and cortisol fill our veins, our bodies ramp up inflammation, and all of the physiological damage is imparted to our body even though this hypothetical event hasn't occurred. But our health is none the wiser, as our bodies believe this was a real event; not a hypothetical scenario.

And in the meantime, we're missing out on every single good thing that God wants to do through us.

Jesus left us with instructions to ward against this destructive mind trap:

"Therefore I tell you, do not worry about your life, what you will eat or drink; or about your body, what you will wear. Is not life more than food, and the body more than clothes? Look at the birds of the air; they do not sow or reap or store away in barns, and yet your heavenly Father feeds them. Are you not much more valuable than they? Can any one of you by worrying add a single hour to your life?

...

... "But seek first his kingdom and his righteousness, and all these things will be given to you as well. Therefore do not worry about tomorrow, for tomorrow will worry about itself. Each day has enough trouble of its own." -Matthew 6:25-27; 33-34

What if we changed our 'what ifs'? What if we asked an entirely different hypothetical?

What if God uses me today?
What if God takes care of all of my needs today?
What if God's will is perfectly done in my life today?
What if I live a full life today?
What if I have the opportunity to love my friends and family today?
What if I'm perfectly healthy today?
What if I have the opportunity to give to someone in need today?
What if I'm able to share the gospel with someone today?

What if I can pray for someone today?
What if I can change someone's life today by something I do or say?
What if something bad does happen to me today, but I get to grow through the process, and become closer to God and more like His Son?

Since we are creatures of habit, this will take some work to retrain our brain. As soon as a negative thought begins to form, we need to stop it in its tracks and invert it into a positive:

"What if I get sick.....hold on. Stop. Let me rephrase that. What if I am perfectly healthy today and I can serve someone?"

This is difficult work. Our natural inclination is to default to negative thoughts, so if we're not consciously aware and paying attention at all times, our mind will inevitably drift to a bad place. The important thing is as soon as we realize that we've gone to that place again, we reverse course and transform our 'what if' to a new 'what if'.

And as we repeat that process over and over, day in and day out, we will learn not to feed our mind with fear. Instead, we will learn to fill our mind with faith.

And Jesus promises us that when we do this, we are building the Kingdom, and God will take care of all of our 'what ifs' along the way.

Worry is faith, but it's the wrong kind of faith. It's faith that God, in the end, cannot take all situations and turn them around for good.

If you find yourself in a state of worry and negative thoughts that are paralyzing you, I encourage you to remember to turn back to this first entry in the book, and read it as many times as necessary. You may need to do it every day, and that's o.k.

I would encourage you to take this section and print it out (take a photo and print it out, type into a word processor and print it out, or write it out by hand). Then tape this to your mirror so that it's the first thing you see in the morning, and the last thing you see before you go to bed.

What if we changed our 'what ifs'?
What if we asked an entirely different hypothetical?

What if God uses me today?
What if God takes care of all of my needs today?
What if God's will is perfectly done in my life today?
What if I live a full life today?
What if I have the opportunity to love my friends and family today?
What if I'm perfectly healthy today?
What if I have the opportunity to give to someone in need today?
What if I'm able to share the gospel with someone today?
What if I can pray for someone today?
What if I can change someone's life today by something I do or say?
What if something bad does happen to me today, but I get to grow through the process and become closer to God and more like His Son?

Build

It's much easier to stop something than it is to start something.

I can easily tell you one thousand ways to make hair stop growing.

But, can I find one thousand ways to make hair start growing? It's very difficult to find just one way.

It's easy to develop a drug that stops an enzyme from working (most drugs work this way). But it's near impossible to discover a drug that will make a broken enzyme start working again.

A while back, my son broke his arm. His arm broke in less than a second, without any thought or action on his part except for accidentally falling. To fix the bone, it required specialized doctors, a wide array of different technologies, a complex biological regenerative system, and 3 months of time. It was much easier for him to break his bone than it was to fix it.

It's the same with our view on life. It's very easy to find the wrong in someone or something. It's easy to complain. It's easy to come up with excuses in our mind of why something won't work.

It's very easy to find ways to be pessimistic. It's very easy to list all of the things wrong with someone else.

It's also very easy to sit back and do nothing with our lives.

The universe is hardwired to be negative. It's the easy path. Due to our good friend entropy, destroying something is much easier than creating something.

But in the midst of entropy, crystals still form from dust. DNA still replicates and creates beautiful biological structures. Planets still orbit in perfect elliptical synchrony. This reverse in entropy is possible because of directed energy from the mind of God.

Escaping our natural tendency to be negative is difficult. But it can be done if we direct the right energy.

An employee will tell you the 99 ways why something can't be done. An entrepreneur will tell you the one way that it can.

Learn to build rather than destroy.
Learn to lift up rather than tear down.
Learn to be optimistic rather than pessimistic.
Learn to find things to be thankful for rather than complain.
Learn to find the good in someone else rather than itemizing their faults.
Learn to have faith rather than doubt.
And use whatever gifts God has given to you to create something new.

We ought to spend our time creating rather than complaining.

It may be a song. It may be a writing. It may be a dress. It may be a photo. It may be a painting. It may be a cake or brownie for someone else. The point is, we can all create because we were all made in the image of God, and God is a creator. And everything we create can be used to love others, glorify God, and build the Kingdom.

Ask God how He wants you to build with your life. Shift your focus from negative to positive.

There's much work to be done, and the naysayers aren't the ones who are going to do it.

It's time to build.

Anytime You Want

Pick any CEO of a major company, and ask how long it would take for you to get on their calendar to have a conversation with them. Even if you were lucky enough to have them agree to speak with you, how much of their time would they give you?

I remember a time that I really wanted a meeting with the CEO of GlaxoSmithKline. I knew I had absolutely no chance of such a thing happening because he didn't know me from Adam, and I was a nobody. I had no connections to him. So, I decided that I would guess what his email address was, and I sent off a short email that said I'd like to have a meeting with him. I really didn't expect that I would be granted a chance to meet him, or that he would even read it, but I thought it was worth a shot.

A short time later, I received a response to the email. The CEO wanted to meet with me. I think I did a few karate kicks, punches in the air, dance moves, head banging, and air guitar moves privately in my office after I read the email. My antics were akin to the level of passion exuberated by none other than Dwight K. Schrute.

I showed up at his penthouse office at the agreed upon date and time. As I sat in the waiting area, I saw his picture on the front of a magazine on a table. It all felt surreal. I had no clue why this man decided to meet with me, without knowing who I was, or even why I wanted to talk to him.

He exited his office and came out to greet me, and then he invited me into his office. I sat down on a couch with him, and he looked at me and said, "you have 15 minutes."

After me bumbling through my presentation, he picked up his phone, called the head of R&D and told him that he wanted him to meet with me. He then ended the meeting by heading out on a flight.
I think I did a few more karate kicks and air punches in the parking garage.

I was praying to God one day and speaking honestly with Him. I thought to myself, "what a privilege to be able to talk to the creator of the entire universe, anytime I want, for as long as a I want, without winning the email lottery and being granted a 15 minute-once-in-a-lifetime-appointment."

Why don't I celebrate with joy the same way I did that day? Why do I take it for granted like it's some chore or responsibility?

THE CREATOR OF THE UNIVERSE WILL TALK TO ME ANYTIME I WANT, FOR AS LONG AS I WANT, AS MANY TIMES AS I WANT, WITHOUT AN APPOINTMENT!!!!

And the creator of the universe is certainly more powerful, more important, MORE WORTH TALKING TO, than any CEO.

And guess what?

THE CREATOR OF THE UNIVERSE WILL TALK TO YOU ANYTIME YOU WANT, FOR AS LONG AS YOU WANT, AS MANY TIMES AS YOU WANT, WITHOUT AN APPOINTMENT!!!!

What an amazing privilege, and I would dare say that many of us take this extraordinary gift completely for granted.

This was all made possible by the sacrifice of Jesus on the cross. Every single one of us can access God directly! The veil was torn in two.

Please, don't live your entire life taking this for granted.

You don't need to send an email to a random address hoping you got it right. You don't have to be lucky, rich, influential, or important. You don't need a special connection to get you an appointment.

He will talk to you, anytime you want, for as long as you want, as many times as you want.

Marcy

One morning, my friend Brian sent me a YouTube video titled "Marcy." I decided to listen to the video on the drive home from work one evening. The video is about how a man had a divine encounter with a lady named Marcy while flying on a commercial airplane, which then led to several other miracles on the flight.

About 15 minutes into the video, I passed a small house on the right that had a small yard sale in front. I felt God tugging to turn around and go to the yard sale.

So, I turned around and pulled into the driveway of a small, rundown house. I started to look through the items, and then a man named Rashad came out to meet me. I thought perhaps God had sent me there to talk to Rashad, so I began asking him questions about his life as I checked out the different items for sale. I learned that he was having trouble making ends meet and had 5 children and a wife. I felt that God was asking me to buy some items to help him out, so I picked up a set of golf clubs and an old jewelry box.

I asked Rashad if I could pray for him, and he told me his lower back was in pain. After praying for his back to be healed, I went to the car to get the money. I thought that meeting Rashad was the reason I was supposed to be there. I also met his uncle.

As I turned around to hand the money to Rashad, I was surprised to see an older lady standing there about three feet from me. It seemed like she appeared out of nowhere. She had long hair and was wearing a long T-shirt. She was puffing on a vape and she had an orange stain on her chin. She was quiet and just stared at me with intensity.

I asked her for her name.

She replied, "Marcy."

I said, "Wait, did you just say your name was Marcy?"

She replied, "Yes."

I said, "That's really strange, I was just listening to a video about a lady named Marcy as I was driving past your house, and I felt God telling me to turn around and come here, but I didn't know why. Now I find you, and your name is Marcy. Do you know why God would send me here?"

She replied that she didn't know. She continued to stare at me with intensity.

I said, "Is there something you need?"

She replied, "not that I know of. I mean, I guess I could use some money."

So, I asked her if she had a job, and she said that she didn't because she didn't have transportation and needed a car.

I said, "I'm going to give you some money, but I feel there's some bigger reason I'm here."

As I stared into her eyes, I felt the presence of God come upon me and I felt like I was staring into the eyes of Jesus, and her face was like looking into the face of Jesus. It was overwhelming.

As I continued to look into her eyes, I said to her, "When I look into your eyes, I see the eyes of Jesus. It's like I'm looking at Jesus right now. I think He sent me here because He wants you to know that He loves you very much."

She then opened up to me and started telling me about how her son had passed away when he was 19 from an infection he got at the hospital. She told me that he had Cerebral Palsy growing up, and then he died suddenly.

At that moment, I felt God talking through me and I told her that what had happened to her son wasn't God's intention, and that her son is happy now and he is ok. I told her again how much Jesus loves her.

As I was telling her this, her eyes started filling with tears and she started crying.

Afterward, she told me she has diabetes and uses insulin. I prayed for her that this would be healed. As we were praying, I felt a hand on my shoulder. Rashad had came over to pray with us.

I drove past that home for years. I never stopped.

But that one day, I did. And now I have a set of golf clubs that I'll probably never use, and a jewelry box that's missing 3 drawers that I gave to my wife when I got home.

It was a divine encounter because my friend Brian listened to God and sent me that video. If he didn't, I would have never pressed in. God orchestrated the entire thing.

When you feel God tugging, listen. Take risks.

There are millions of people like Marcy all around us. If you go out on a limb, I think you'll find that God was already on the end of the limb ready to meet you there.

Our True Idol

I've found that there's one idol at the heart of all of my other idols.

It's easy to do an accounting to identify and list out all of our idols - those things that are external to ourselves that we place extraordinary value upon, and to stand them up and scream, "You blasted idol! You're evil!"

Once we externalize our idols and view them as outside forces that we have been victimized by because of our weakness, we have been fooled. This process diverts our attention away from the real problem.

Our heart.

If we synthesize fake boogie men, we're never forced to deal with the root cause of our problem.

An idol is anything that is worth more to us than God.

We may claim that our comfort is an idol.
Our career.
Money.
Material possessions.
Pleasure.
Status.

A person.

There are literally millions of things that can serve as an idol.

But ask yourself the next layer of question. Why is X one of my idols? Why do I hold this thing in such high esteem?

If you are like me, you will find that the answer to that question is, "Because idol X affects ME in such and such a way..." The operative word is "ME". It's all about what that idol does for ME.

 I feel comfortable.
 I feel happy.
 I feel good.
 I feel important.....

So, who is the real idol?

Me!

At the end of the day, we all worship ourselves, not the idols. The idols are just external vehicles for us to worship ourselves.

Let me repeat that because I think this is key:

Our idols are just external vehicles for us to worship ourselves.

We don't like to admit this. We want to minimize our guilt by setting up and blaming an external idol.

But all of these idols are nothing more than paper tigers. They are nothing. Vapor.

They are virtual constructs designed to prevent us from recognizing the true source of our problem.

Idols want to stay alive. Idols die hard. One way an idol can protect itself is to fool you into believing that it's not an idol. If the real idol can pass the blame onto any number of fake idols and make you believe that those objects are your enemy, then you'll leave the real idol alone. It gets to survive. The real idol (you) gets to see another day, while you fight a fictitious legion of straw men that have redirected your attention elsewhere.

We need to get smarter. We should focus our attention inward.

This is why Jesus said that out of the heart flows everything else. He pointed out our idol as plain as day. Our heart. This is why we need a new heart. Our heart sits on a throne and needs to be removed.

We don't like to admit that our core value structure is based on the belief that we are more valuable than God. Who would be bold enough to admit that they feel this way? It's much easier to admit that an external idol is more important than God, than it is to admit that we believe ourself to be more important than God.

To bury this hard lesson far from our consciousness, we have placed ourselves at the center of an epic struggle existing between external idols and our willpower to abandon them. That externalization removes our guilty conscience.

It turns out that the only thing we need to abandon is ourself. When we do, all other "idols" are automatically obliterated.

As long as we continue to hopelessly fight fictitious external idols, nothing will ever change. Our heart still sits on the throne while we're busy trying to incinerate paper tigers. Once we can come to terms that we are the ultimate idol, we can get to the real work.

And the real work is this: asking Jesus to replace our heart with a new one.

"The heart is deceitful above all things, and desperately sick; who can understand it?" - Jeremiah 17:9

"For where your treasure is, there your heart will be also." - Matthew 6:21

"These people honor me with their lips, but their hearts are far from me." - Mark 7:6

".....who will bring to light the things now hidden in darkness and will disclose the purposes of the heart." - I Corinthians 4:5

"The good person out of the good treasure of his heart produces good, and the evil person out of his evil treasure produces evil, for out of the abundance of the heart his mouth speaks." - Luke 6:45

"Blessed are the pure in heart, for they will see God." - Matthew 5:8

On Pain and Suffering

Why doesn't God step in and stop all of the evil, pain, and suffering in this world?

Answer: He already has, is, and will. He's just not doing it according to the way man desires.

God's defeat of evil begins and ends at the cross.

And now the gospel is working out that defeat over both time and space.

God's ways are not our ways. His process will lead to much better results in the long run than man's plan to instantaneously fix things magically by snapping our fingers. Man wants instantaneous gratification and comfort without sacrifice or cost.

Our focus is on timing, while God's focus is on process. Humans are like the employees that demand a year's wages after they haven't shown up to work all year.

Humans demand limitless freedom and refuse to be controlled, but then they demand that God control people by intervening to stop evil. We can't have it both ways. Do you want to be free, or do you want God to control people?

God is playing a game of chess against evil, not in two dimensions or three dimensions, but in infinite dimensions. He's outsmarting evil at every turn. Like a master jujitsu artist, all evil is being leveraged for good.

We don't have to understand every detail of God's plan to know that the ultimate outcome is good. We may think we know how to do things better, but our methods would result in disaster.

If God can take the evil that was in the hearts of men who crucified Jesus and turn it into the salvation of mankind, I have faith that He can take any of our bad situations and turn it into something good.

All evil will be used for good.

We can have faith and place our hope in that promise.

———————————

"And we know that in all things God works for the good of those who love him, who have been called according to his purpose." – Romans 8:28

"But as for you, you meant evil against me; but God meant it for good, in order to bring it about as it is this day, to save many people alive." — Genesis 50:20

The Living Truth

When Jesus claims that He is the "Way, the Truth, and the Life," what does He mean?

We tend to have this idea of the truth being this sterile, objective, external list of do's and don'ts.

We do not assign a personality to the truth, because we tend to think of the truth as this static law which is completely void of a personality. In fact, the more impartial, the better.

In our way of thinking, if a list of rules and regulations could be developed for every scenario, there's no need for a personality to be involved. To us, the truth is algorithmic. An equation. A great big list of "If this, then that's." We have this notion that the truth should be able to be recorded and interpreted by a computer.

When Christ entered the world, He turned this notion on its head. He obliterated the concept of the cold law, and taught us that the Truth is living and dynamic - that the Truth has a personality. He taught us that the Truth is infused with emotion and great Love, and that it's certainly anything but algorithmic.

We believe the truth says, "They ought to be stoned!"

Jesus taught us that the Truth says, "Let he who is without sin pick up the first stone."

We believe the truth says, "If someone wrongs you, they should be brought to justice."

Jesus said, "if someone strikes you on one cheek, turn to them the other..."

We believe the truth says, "There is a limit to the number of times we should forgive someone."

Jesus said, "There is no end to forgiveness."

We believe the truth says, "Only if you actually carry out the act, are you fully guilty of it."

Jesus said, "Even if you think it in your mind, you are guilty of it."

We believe the truth says, "You must die for that."

Jesus said, "I will die for you."

Jesus challenged every algorithm. He taught us that you can't build a formula around the Truth. The real Truth defies our attempts to logically compartmentalize and formalize the law. We can't really nail it down. We can't turn it into a science. We just know it when we see it.

Why? Why must this be so? Why can't the truth just be this external, objective, standard?

To answer that question, answer this question first - where did the Truth come from in the first place?

Did the truth exist as this standalone, external thing that God then incorporated into His character? Or, does the truth originate from God?

In Plato's "Euthyphro", Socrates presents this question to Euthyphro in what is commonly called, "Euthyphro's dilemma" which asks (paraphrased): "Does God command morals because they are good, or are the commands of God moral because He commands them?"

I believe the answer is neither.

The Truth and God are one in the same.

And because God is a living being with a personality, so is the Truth.

And because Jesus and the Father are one, He was able to claim, "I am the Way, The Truth, and the Life."

This is why Jesus taught us that all of the Law is summarized by loving God and loving others. He was showing us that the Truth is always motivated by Love, and that Love is expressed by a personality, not writing on a piece of paper.

The Truth is not a defined list.
The Truth is a living person.
Get to know Him, and you will know the Truth.

That's why the Truth will set you free.
Jesus, the person, sets you free.

Not a system of rules.

A list of rules only serves in a capacity to reveal to you that you need the Truth.

And you when you discover that you need the Truth, you find Him waiting there to welcome you with open arms.

How Do You Know True Faith?

People act on true faith.

Now, please grant me a little leniency as I use the word "faith" in a metaphorical sense to relate to theologically defined faith.

If I have faith that a plane can take me from point A to point B, then I will take action and ride on the plane.

If I have faith that food has calories that will enable me to live another day, then I will take action and eat food.

If I have faith that water will clean my body, then I will take action and take a shower.

If I have faith that a surgery will fix my body, then I'll take action and instruct the doctor to perform surgery on me.

If I have faith that a poison will kill me, then I will take action and do everything within my power to keep the poison from entering my body.

However, if I am under the illusion that I believe something, and I have never taken action on it, it is nothing more than an untested theory. What exists in my mind exists in the land of the theoretical.

For theory to transform into faith, it needs to be tested, and to test something, we need to take action by assuming it is true and then by acting accordingly. And when we test the theory and discover its truthfulness, it will transform into faith. And this faith will result in continued and perpetual action, the same kind of continued action as eating food every day.

If the thought in my mind never translates into real action, it will never escape the theoretical zone.

Nonetheless, it is quite commonplace for people to assume that faith simply means mentally agreeing with a premise, and nothing more.

We study the premise. We theorize about the premise. We read about the premise. We have bible studies about the premise. We watch videos and read blogs about the premise. We tell others about the premise and tell them to study the premise. We dissect the premise into layers of increasing detail, and turn it into a philosophical science.

And we call that faith.

Not so. It is still just a theory. Until we act upon it and test it, it is nothing but a vapor in our mind; nothing but a sophisticated academic exercise.

If you want real faith, act. And real faith will compel us to act.

Remember Peter? What did Jesus ask Peter to do? Jesus asked Peter to come out of the boat and walk on the water in the middle of a storm.

Peter had witnessed Jesus walking on water. Peter had witnessed Jesus perform other miracles, And Peter knew that Jesus was trustworthy from witnessing repeated examples of trustworthiness. Even with all of this knowledge, Peter only THEORETICALLY knew that he could walk on water. In Peter's mind, this was nothing but a theory with a high probability of being true.

What was Peter lacking? He was lacking action that tested that belief.

And when he stepped out of that boat, Peter transformed theory into practice, and belief became faith.

Have you stepped out of the boat yet?

"For as the body apart from the spirit is dead, so also faith apart from works is dead." - James 2:26

Does God Feel Distant and Silent?

"Where in the world is God?," you may be asking right now in your life.

Sometimes we get into a deep rut where we feel God is far away from us. We hear nothing but complete silence. Sometimes it almost feels as if He just spun the universe into existence and then left the scene to let things run on autopilot. Every now and then He might peak His head inside to see if we've blown ourselves up yet.

Ever feel that way? Like you're just going through the motions and grinding your gears in a 'godless' existence?

Let's reason together and think through this for a moment.

God never changes.
Given this truth, if He was close to us at one point and now He isn't, is it because He changed?

God is immovable.
Given this truth, if He was close to us at one point and now He isn't, is it because He moved?

God is holding the entire universe together, every second of every day. Given this truth, if God felt present at one point and now He doesn't, is it because He stopped holding the universe together?

God sent His one and only Son to die for us so that He could have a personal, intimate relationship with us.
Given this truth, if He loved us that much 2,000 years ago, did He just randomly change His mind?

God sent His Holy Spirit to live directly inside of us.
Given this truth, if God feels far away from us, is it because the Holy Spirit decided to quit?

When we consider the above, it appears that if God feels distant it's not because He decided to take a long vacation.

God doesn't change.
God is immovable.
God is holding every atom in our body together.
God loves us.
God wants to have a relationship with us, and God made a way for that to happen.

So, by process of elimination, if God feels distant, it's because WE'RE distant.

"Draw near to God, and He will draw near to you." - James 4:8

"Here I am! I stand at the door and knock. If anyone hears my voice and opens the door, I will come in and eat with that person, and they with me." - Revelation 3:20

*"Jesus replied, "Anyone who loves me will obey my teaching. My Father will love them, and we will come to them and make our home with them." -*John 14:23

Sounds like the ball is in our court, doesn't it?

When we get to that point in our life where God feels distant, that is the litmus test that alerts us to the fact that we've been drifting away from God.

Einstein taught us that motion is relative. A car running into a cement wall at 60 mph is identical to that same wall moving at 60 mph into the stationary car. Conversely, a spaceship moving away from the sun is equivalent to the sun moving away from the ship.

If you were in a spaceship and could see nothing else but the sun, and your ship was drifting away from the sun, and you looked out of your window, what would you see? You would see the sun moving away from you!!!

And you would ask, "Why is the sun moving away from me?"

You would quickly realize (being the smart astronaut that you are), that the sun hasn't moved a centimeter. You're the one moving away. But because of your reference frame in the weightlessness of space, it didn't feel like you were moving at all!

It's the same with us and God. If it "appears" God has drifted away while we were left fending for ourselves in the void of darkness, it's really because we've been drifting away from God.

And just like the inside of that ship, sometimes it's hard to ascertain or sense that we're the one who has been drifting. It's easy to go throughout the motions of our day on autopilot, while not realizing that we have been silently but surely moving away from God the entire time.

A drift can occur very slowly; slow enough that we hardly realize it.

When we finally take a moment to pause and find the sun, we see it's no longer a magnificent thermonuclear sphere taking up the entire field of view of the window. It's a tiny point of light, so small in fact that it just disappears into the star field so that we no longer can identify which star is the sun.

We cry out, "Where did you go, God? Please come back."

God cries out, "I'm right here. I have been the entire time. You have been drifting away, and I've been calling you back. Please come home, my child."

Does God feel far right now?

The good news is that He's not as far as you realize, and He is calling you home.

Who is the Gospel For?

We all desperately hope for evil to be destroyed and all things to be made new in this evil world around us.........

.......until we learn that the same thing needs to happen within us.

We all want evil to vanish, until we realize that it's evil within us that needs to be destroyed.

We all want pornography and sex trafficking to end, until we realize that it's the lustful thoughts within us that needs to end.

We all want racism to end, until we realize that it's pride within us that needs to end.

We all want justice in this world, until we realize that we also need to be held accountable for every evil thought or action, even the secret ones that nobody else knows about.

The gospel is not about "destroying all the evil out there."

The gospel is not about the "evil in the world."

First and foremost, the gospel is about ME.

Jesus came to destroy the evil in MY heart.

It's true that Jesus' death on the cross was to deal with every form of evil everywhere, but if we focus our attention on destroying the "evil out there", we neglect the fact that there is much evil within us that needs to be dealt with first.

When Jesus came to this earth, He proclaimed from the rooftops, "The kingdom of Heaven is here! The kingdom of God is here!"

He didn't say, "Don't worry, the kingdom of God will be here in a couple thousand years. For now, let's make do with what we've got. In the meantime, let me entertain you with some miracles."

Take a moment and look around you. Do you see the kingdom of heaven here on earth now?

I don't. Did Jesus lie? No, absolutely not.

Why? Because the kingdom of God is here inside of me! It's available to me right now. "All" things being made new means that the "all" within me is being made new.

When Jesus taught us how to pray, what did He tell us to pray for? Jesus taught us to pray that God's will be done on earth as it is in heaven.

How does this happen? How does God's will take place on this earth?

We find the answer to this question by asking, "Who lives on this earth?"

Well, we do.
I do.

You do.

We all do.

So, the only way God's will occurs on earth as it does in heaven is if heaven lives within me right now.

We need to start focusing on the changes that desperately need to happen within us. Our flesh needs to die every single day.

We need to focus on letting God build the kingdom of heaven within us.

Wait, correction......"I" need to start focusing on the changes that desperately need to happen within "ME". My flesh needs to die every single day.

"I" need to focus on letting God build the kingdom of Heaven within "ME."

I need to stop thinking externally, and to start thinking internally.

As the Gospel makes me into a new person, then I, in turn, can let the Gospel flow through me to work in others.

But the Gospel starts with me.

A Speck of Faith

Jesus told us that if we have faith, even in the tiniest amount, that we will be able to tell a mountain to move, and it will move.

A mountain is only a mountain because we perceive it to be a mountain. If we were to move back one hundred miles from the mountain, the mountain would now be a tiny speck. Conversely, if we were to magnify a speck of sand one million times, it would quickly become a mountain.

So, either Jesus is telling us that the mountain will actually move, or He is telling us that our faith will change our perception about the mountain.

I'm reminded of a photograph depicting a horse that is strapped to a small, flimsy plastic chair that weighs less than five pounds. The horse isn't moving because the horse believes it is strapped to something that's immovable.

Sometimes, like this horse, we can't move - not because of a real physical limitation - but because we lack the belief that moving is even a possibility. We lack the faith to move, that's all. The problem is all about our perception, and our perception is governed by our faith, or lack thereof.

In the sense that they prevent us from moving, the limitations that our mind places on us are real. In the sense that they take over our thoughts and cause worry, the problems that our mind invents are real. But they cease being real when our perception changes due to faith.

Jesus said that all of the needs of the birds are taken care of, even though they don't labor and worry about their problems. In a sense, a bird is like a child- it doesn't perceive that it has any problems, therefore, it doesn't have any problems. If the bird were to somehow convince itself that its next meal may be impossible to find, and the bird begins to imagine every possible scenario of how things could go wrong, it would suddenly have problems that it didn't have before.

Jesus tells us to have the faith of a child. The type of faith that doesn't invent problems where there aren't any, or that magnifies specks into mountains.

This same principle is evident in the laws of physics. If there's anything that Einstein's theory of relativity teaches us, it's that time, space, and matter are all gauged by our perception. Light (God) is absolute, but everything else changes in relation to our frame of reference.

I'm not claiming that some people don't have real problems; however, I am asking this: how many problems are just a figment of our imagination due to lack of faith?

Notice, the only way the immobilized horse remains chained to this self-imposed problem is to never move an inch. The horse must remain absolutely still. For if the horse moved its body but a hair's length, he would see the chair move, and once the horse became aware that the chair moved in response to his tiny effort, its fictitious hold on him would become no more. The chair would cease being a mountain in the mind of the horse.

The horse only needs a speck of faith to move. For us, this is very good news. Many of our problems are simply a tiny movement away from vanishing.

—————————————————

"He replied, "Because you have so little faith. Truly I tell you, if you have faith as small as a mustard seed, you can say to this mountain, 'Move from here to there,' and it will move. Nothing will be impossible for you." – Matthew 17:20

Unchanging Love

One of the foundational characteristics of God is His immutability. God remains the same across all dimensions of His character. God is not subject to the flow of time, and all change is coupled to time.

Since everything about God never changes, this naturally includes His love for us. We know that 2000 years ago, His love was of such magnitude that He was willing to give His one and only Son so that we might live.

Since He never changes, His love never changes. And since His love never changes, we know that the greatness of His love for us today is the same as it was 2000 years ago.

His willingness to forgive is the same.
His willingness to save is the same.
His willingness to sacrifice everything for us is the same.

God loves us with the same love He loved us with two millennia ago. And since His love never changes, there is absolutely nothing we can ever do to cause God to lose His love for us. His love is not contingent on our performance, or lack thereof.

Fully grasping and believing this truth is life changing. It sets you free to serve God with all of your heart, mind, soul, and strength - because you know that He will love you even if you fail.

"For God so loved the world, that he gave his only begotten Son, that whosoever believeth in him should not perish, but have everlasting life." – John 3:16

The Physical Can't Stop the Spiritual

"Take a guard," Pilate answered. "Go, make the tomb as secure as you know how." So they went and made the tomb secure by putting a seal on the stone and posting the guard." - Matthew 27:65-66

Well, as hard as they tried to make sure Jesus remained dead, it didn't work. They sealed the tomb, and they guarded the tomb around the clock. They thought they had covered all of their bases, and from a physical standpoint, they had.

The only problem was that the miracle that was about to take place was spiritual, and you can't muster up enough physical resources or weapons to stop what is destined to take place in the spiritual.

Jesus rose from the dead at the appointed time and place, even though every weapon of man was used to prevent it from happening.

In the same way that Jesus was made alive in the tomb of death, Christ will be made alive in every dead person who invites Him in. It's inevitable.

New Life will spring up at the appointed time and place within that person, and they will be made new.

If the Spirit lives in a person, they will produce good fruit.

Their life will be transformed and made new in the spiritual sense.

It's inevitable.

God's Word will not return void. It will accomplish what it was set to do, regardless of any effort by man or devil to stop it.

In the same way, the Spirit will work in you to produce a new person.

In the same way that God wants the gospel to spread to every corner of the planet, God wants the gospel to spread to every corner of your heart, soul, and mind.

In the same way that God wants to make disciples of all nations, God wants to make every area of your life a disciple.

In the same way God wants to save every person, God wants to save every area of your life.

In the same way that God so loved the world that He gave His one and only Son, God so loved you that He gave His one and only Son.

In the same way that God lives in Christ, God will live in you to make you a person who loves others, forgives their enemies, and who produces good fruit.

And if the Spirit truly lives in you, then nothing in the physical realm can stop this transformation.

Just like the physical couldn't stop Jesus from rising from the dead.

Don't Get to the End of Your Life

Don't get to the end of your life and find out that the kingdom you were building your entire life turned out to be the wrong one.

Don't get to the end of your life and discover that the kingdom you were building is all for naught and will vanish the moment you do.

Don't get to the end of your life holding a bag of regrets of how you spent your time and what you valued.

Remember, God gave us each a certain degree of resources and talents. Some one, some five, and some ten. Use whatever you have (time, resources, and talents) to build the right kingdom. Don't build your own kingdom, someone else's kingdom, or the world's kingdom.

Those who love their life in this world will lose it, but those who give up their life for Christ will find it.

If you spend your resources building God's kingdom, you will have no regrets when you leave this planet, and all of the work you did will be waiting on you at your next destination.

Giving up the temporary to inherit the eternal sounds like a pretty good deal to me. If I do the math, that's an interest rate of infinity.

Did You?

Did you create space, matter, time, and energy, all of which provide you with the framework for existence?
A: No

Did you create the quirky laws of quantum physics that make it possible for you to live in a deterministic universe, while leaving you with free will?
A: No

Did you create the earth, and all its ecosystems to make life possible on the planet?
A: No

Did you create the sun, a sustainable thermonuclear reaction one million times the size of the earth, positioned precisely at 93 million miles away to provide the planet with just the right amount of energy?
A: No

Did you create the laws of biochemistry and molecular biology so that one cell could become the 30 trillion cells in your body, with each cell differentiating into its specific location and function in the body?
A: No

Did you create the 3 billion letters of code in your DNA which provide the blueprints for creating the human body?

A: No

Did you create the law of gravity with perfect balance such that you wouldn't be crushed or float off the earth into outer space?
A: No

Did you create the 100 trillion neural connections in the human brain, perfectly mapped out to create cognition, thought, logic, reason, language, emotions, perceptions, and control over the other 30 trillion cells in the body?
A: No

So, what did you do?
A: Nothing

How much credit do you deserve?
A: None

Why do you live your life as if you're the master of your own destiny and that you're at the center of the universe?
A: I don't know.

What right do you have to tell Me how to do My job?
A: None

Why do you wake up day after day, never giving Me credit or thanking Me, and taking everything around you for granted?
A: I don't know.

Who left His heavenly realm and wrapped Himself in human flesh to show you how to live?
A: You.

Who felt the pain of watching His one and only Son die so that you could be completely absolved of all sin?
A: You did.

Who raised His life from the grave, so that you could also be raised from the grave to new life?
A: You.

So, what right do you have to tell me that I don't love you?
A: None.

What right do you have to tell me that I don't understand what it's like to experience the pain of being human, sin, and death?
A: None.

Where does that leave you, oh wise and self-sufficient one?
A: My life, oh God, is completely in Your hands.

Joy

The thing about circumstances is that they always change.

The thing about God is that He never changes.

So, I need to ask myself this very important question - do I want my joy to be in a constant state of flux, or do I want my joy to be a constant?

If I want my joy to fluctuate, then I will base my joy on my circumstances.

If I want my joy to be immune to change, then I will base my joy on God.

If my joy depends on my circumstances, then my circumstances are my god.

If my joy depends on God, then God is my God.

Does God Still Love Me Today?

In what ways has God demonstrated His love for me today?

We all have this notion that God created the universe as an autonomous, self-sustaining system - sort of like He wound it up, let it go, and now He just sits back while the universe runs itself on automatic, and He chooses when He will (or will not) externally intervene at certain points.

Nothing could be further from the truth. From His Word, we know that He sustains all things, and He holds all things together. From our understanding of quantum physics, we now see why this is necessary.

Every quark, photon, electron, subatomic particle, energy field, and force is continually being sustained and held together by God.

Even the fabric of spacetime is being held together by God.

If at any second God chooses to remove His sustaining power, everything would immediately cease to exist.

This means that if we are still living this very moment, it's only because God made a conscious decision to sustain our existence this moment.

Our existence is not the downstream result of God taking His hands off the wheel and letting the universe run itself. Instead, God is making a conscious decision at every moment to sustain the universe and hold our lives together.

If you took 20,000 breaths today, it's only because God sustained and held together every molecule that participated in each breath, and the spacetime continuum in which those molecules dwell.

And up to this point, God has made this decision every second of every day of every week of every year of every decade of every century of every millennia.

Our brains won't think the next thought, our hearts won't beat the next beat, and our lungs won't take the next breath unless God specifically and purposefully wills it.

And when that next thought, heartbeat, and breath occurs, God must will the next one for our life to continue.

Every moment exists only because God chooses it to exist. In Him we live and move and have our being (Acts 17:28). This constant sustaining power of God is not only spiritually true, it is literally true in the physical sense.

So, if I'm asking if God showed me His love today, I first need to ask how many seconds He sustained me today. Every one of those seconds was an act of love.

Even in the midst of every act of disobedience, every prideful stance, every lustful thought, every selfish act, every absence of faith, every ungrateful and rebellious attitude, God still chooses to continue my existence each and every second.

And He continues to sustain the entire universe, in the midst of a world that continues to reject Him and spit in His face, even after enduring this same treatment on the cross.

God's mercy and love isn't just shown by His one-time act of sacrifice on the cross; it's shown continually by each ticking second that He CHOOSES to continue our existence, collectively and individually.

How did God show you His love today?

Sand is Not Bland

If you look at sand, what do you see?

When you step back and look from a distance, sand looks pretty much the same, no? Our imaginations understand that trillions of individual sand particles come together to form a pretty uniform picture.

Taken as a whole, it's pretty much the same color and texture throughout. Sand appears, for the most part, quite generic and unremarkable. It's really easy to put sand into the same bucket and just call it "sand."

But what happens if you zoom in and look at individual grains of sand?

We may think that since sand appears uniform at the big scale, that the individual grains of sand ought to be meticulously alike.

(Google 'sand under a microscope', and click on images to see microscopic images of sand.)

Amazingly, if you study sand under a microscope, you find something that is counterintuitive and quite extraordinary— each grain is one-of-a-kind. Every grain is different from any other grain, and not just in size or shade of color, but in fundamental structure and beauty.

It's almost as if each grain is incomparable to any other. Yet, when you zoom back out, sand takes on a prosaic dullness and predictability.

How many of us are like those grains of sand? Society tries to fit us all into the same mold. Culture wants to stereotype us all into the same banal existence, defined by categories that each of us are destined to bear. Society attempts to pigeonhole us, define us, and typecast us into a category that we have no control over.

From birth, we all develop labels that have been pre-designed for us; labels that we were never meant to carry. And all of us, invariably, march to the beat of this droning drum, like faithful soldiers that have all been cast from the same die. We try to fit into the pattern that society has defined for us, so that we can obediently take our position among the endless sea of people that make up human sand.

But did you know that we were not meant for this? Did you know that just like a single grain of sand, you are uniquely and wonderfully made?

God's handprint overshadows society's impulse to standardize you, and exclusively marks out a unique expression of creativity outlined by your you-ness. There is no other creature quite like you—not by a long-shot. You are meant to be matchless, uncommon, and unusual.

And perhaps even harder for us to grasp is the fact that, "so is our neighbor."

Sometimes we can mindlessly join the masses and stereotype everyone else around us into neatly defined buckets of collectiveness. We tend to reduce another person to "one of those people." We tend to, well, make everyone into the same grain of sand.

To stop doing this to ourselves, and to others, we have to take the time to zoom in. We would never know that each sand particle was unique unless we took the time to zoom in and study each grain.

To get to know ourselves and others, we have to take our eyes, hearts, and attention off of the larger worldview and to pay attention to the little things happening all around us. The things that make us uniquely and individually "us."

And when we position our attention relationally instead of culturally, that sterilized, fuzzy image of each person that we have formed through the lens of the social order will come into focus, and we will start to see that we are all, indeed, very special people on an individual level.

We need to resist with all of our might the human tendency to put people into buckets. Although sand was meant to be carried around in a bucket, humans were not. Let us love each person like they are unique, the same way that we believe that we are unique.

This is how we "love" people as Christ taught us.

Christ saw each person as truly special and took the time to recognize their uniqueness. He created each person as if He was starting from scratch.

And just like He gave the gazillions of stars individual names, He gives each one of us a one-of-a-kind name that no one else shares.

Should We Be Surprised?

Should we really be surprised at what we see happening around us today? We shouldn't gasp with surprise; as if all of this is some random unexpected occurrence.

Everything is going exactly according to plan. The current situation and trends we see playing out are precisely what would be expected when people attempt to save themselves.

What we now see is the result of people doing their best to be their own savior - individually and collectively.

Deep down, everyone knows that they need to be saved, and if they reject the true Savior, they only have one option —- which is try like the dickens to save themselves.

This process of self-salvation takes many different forms.

Sometimes it looks like blatant satanism.
Sometimes it looks like unfounded social justice shaming.
Sometimes it looks like greed.
Sometimes it looks like technology.
Sometimes it looks like workaholism.
Sometimes it looks like hyper-sexualization.
Sometimes it looks like deconstruction of every single societal norm.
And, yes, sometimes it looks like hyper-religion.

When man attempts to save himself, it can look evil, and it can look good.

Regardless of how it looks, the one common element is the absence of the one and only true Savior, Jesus Christ.

When Adam and Eve ate the forbidden fruit, they weren't just simply disobeying God. In that act, they were effectively telling God that they desired to be their own saviors.

Ironically, as society continues to try and save itself, the exact opposite will occur. The entire thing will decay at an ever-accelerating rate and will eventually self-destruct.

So, let's not point our fingers at every evil we see and say, "Can you believe how evil these people are!"

Instead, let's think of ways that we can contribute to solving the problem. The ONLY solution is the gospel of Jesus Christ. People need new hearts, and when they are given a new heart, they will stop doing evil.

If we tell people they need to stop doing evil while not sharing the solution, we are contributing to their demise, because we are essentially reaffirming to them that they need to be their own savior.

Not only that; we've told them that they have essentially failed at being their own savior and to please try harder. How pointless and frustrating is that?

First things first.

First is the gospel.

We should focus on the gospel, not on all of the evil you we see around us. If we don't, those who don't know the gospel surely won't focus on the gospel, and they will just continue to do what they think is best, which is to save themselves.

We need to spread the GOOD news. We need to tell people to repent and believe the gospel, for the kingdom of God is here.

Now is not the time to be surprised about what we see happening around us. The evil heart of man was known from before time began.

What we need to focus on now is illuminating the darkness with the Light of God.

God gave us a voice.

God gave us resources.

How can we use them to spread the good news?

Time is short.

Our Time Horizon

I believe one of the constant struggles between God and man is caused by the extreme differences in timescales we are each focused on.

We are naturally inclined to set our time horizon to an infinitesimally small window.

We're focused on the here and now. This is human nature.

God's time horizon is set to infinity. God cares about eternity.

Now, God is working all things with His time horizon as the centerpiece. Everything He does is focused on optimizing something of eternal value and significance. He weighs everything on the scales of eternity to determine its worth.

We, on the other hand, are working all things to benefit the temporary. Our goal is to make our finite time horizon as pleasing as possible. We weigh everything on the scales of today to determine its worth.

We measure the goodness of something by how it maximizes things within our time frame.

God measures the goodness of something by how it maximizes eternity.

Because those two time horizons are separated by an infinite gap, it's almost always the case that something that is deemed worthy in one time frame is deemed counterproductive in the other. This tension will always exist between the two different reference frames.

Things that maximize pleasure in the here and now tend to negatively impact eternity, and likewise, things that bring about a pleasant eternity tend to appear detrimental to the temporal.

This is why we don't like suffering and why we can't see the value in suffering. We don't even like being inconvenienced.

This is why we have extreme difficulty understanding the purpose of evil. And this is why it seems that God may be raining on our parade.

For us both to come into alignment, we need to see through the other's time horizon.

God reached in and experienced our time horizon by wrapping Himself in flesh and entering into the finite. God can see both the present and eternity. He can empathize with us, but His eyes are still set on the ultimate prize of eternity.

Now it's our turn. We need to change our perception to focus on eternity. We need to measure the worth of everything through this lens.

If our perception was transformed to measure eternity rather than the here and now, many of the questions of "why?" would disappear.

We would be able to accept an event or circumstance that affects us in a negative way now, if we understood that it would ultimately have a net positive value in eternity.

Many of our motivations, plans, goals, and desires would radically change. The way we respond to circumstances and current events would completely change.

We would be more in tune with understanding what God is doing on the macro-scale as we become less focused on the micro-scale.

How would it change your life if you removed your temporary lenses and exchanged them for ones that can view eternity?

The Wildest Extremes

We have a special place in the universe, as humans sit in the middle of the wildest extremes of the scale of existence.

The smallest distance is thought to be the Planck length, which is on the order of 1×10^{-35} meters. (0. followed by 34 zeros and then a '1').

This is 100 billionth of a trillionth of a trillionth of a meter.

The largest known size is the observable size of the universe, which is 1×10^{27} meters (1 followed by 27 zeros).

This is 1000 trillion trillion meters. Light traveling from one end of the observable universe would take 93 billion years to reach the other end.

So, the largest thing is 1×10^{62} (1 followed by 62 zeros) bigger than the smallest thing. This is a dynamic size range of 100 trillion trillion trillion trillion trillion.

And the size of humans sits in the middle of these vast extremes at ~2 meters.

The ratio of the size of a human to the smallest thing is 100 million times larger than the ratio of the size of the universe to the size of a human.

Therefore, humans are like 100 million universes compared to the smallest thing!

Our minds are designed such that we can't fathom the smallest thing, and we can't fathom the largest thing.

If we look to the small, we ought to be in awe in equal proportion to when we study the large.

Yet, here we are situated perfectly between these incomprehensible vast extremes in scale.

God shows His grace towards us by making us the perfect size to appreciate both extremes of His creation.

God's Unconditional Love

I believe that the reason we have trouble fully comprehending the truth that God can unconditionally love someone while maintaining hatred of their sin, is because we, ourselves, have trouble separating the two.

Humans equate other humans with their sin, as if those two things are inextricable.

We believe this unspoken notion that people are only as good as their ability to not sin. For this same reason, we have trouble loving people without precondition, and we have trouble forgiving people because we identify people with their sin.

When Christ died, he took all of our sin upon Himself, thereby separating us from our sin.

This act decoupled humanity from sin. God can view a person completely independent from their sin. A person's sin does not bias God's view of that person.

As humans, however, we find it almost impossible to not let someone's sin influence our ability to unconditionally love them.

We project their sin onto their core identity. We allow a person's sin to permanently contaminate our view of them.

Because we have this tendency, we automatically assume that God must possess this same tendency. And because we believe God connects the sin with the sinner, we automatically project God's judgement onto that person.

Personally, we all assume and hope that God treats our sin separately from His love for us. We want God to afford us the benefit of the doubt, and to not hold our sin against us. But, when we view others, we insist that the two be irreversibly connected.

We should learn to adopt God's practice of despising sin, but loving the sinner. This truth readily flows from our lips, but in practice we deny its power.

This is what it means to love others the same way we love ourselves.

If we expect our own worth to God to be the same regardless of our shortcomings, then we should treat and view others with this same consideration.

Your Worth

Your worth is not found in how beautiful you are.
Your worth is not found in how much money you have.
Your worth is not found in how successful you are.
Your worth is not found in how intelligent you are.
Your worth is not found in how influential you are.
Your worth is not found in how many friends you have.
Your worth is not found in how many degrees you have.
Your worth is not found in all of your accomplishments.
Your worth is not found in how much weight you lose.
Your worth is not found in how much hair you have.
Your worth is not found in what kind of car you drive.
Your worth is not found in the size of your home.
Your worth is not found in how cute your children are.
Your worth is not found in your political affiliation.
Your worth is not found in how much work you get done today.
Your worth is not found in your title at work.
Your worth is not found in how stylish your clothes are.
Your worth is not found in how many people like you or love you.

Your worth is found in one thing, and one thing alone.
Jesus.

Your life has incredible worth just by virtue of you being you.

Regardless of any of those other factors listed above, Jesus proclaimed that your life has infinite worth by choosing to die on the cross for your sins.

His choice to die for your sins was not attached to any of the factors listed above.

Not one of them.

They never even came across His radar screen.

End of story.

I have incredible worth.
You have incredible worth.
We all have incredible worth.

Your worth can't be added to by your success.
Your worth can't be reduced by your failures.
Your worth is defined by Jesus Christ.

He has called us friend.
He has washed our feet.
He has paid the ultimate price for us.... His life.

You play no role in increasing or decreasing your worth.

How would your life change if you really, truly, honestly, whole-heartedly, believed this without question?

Don't Let The Crop Go To Waste

Jesus said, "I tell you, open your eyes and look at the fields! They are ripe for harvest." - John 4:35

What happens to a crop that is ripe for harvest if it isn't harvested?

It falls back into the ground and it dies.

This is hard truth to swallow, but I really can't think of anything more wasteful.

This is exactly what will happen if we don't go into the fields and work.

Why aren't we working in the fields?

Perhaps it's because we haven't taken the first step. Jesus said the first step is to open our eyes and look at the fields. If we aren't looking, we will completely miss that there is a field all around us that's ready to harvest.

This is what happens when we ignore the world around us.

Where are these fields? Where do we go to look for them?

Fields are everywhere around us. Look ten feet in front of wherever you're standing right now, and there's a field.

The store.
The parking lot.
The restaurant.
Work.
The park.
The sidewalk.
Your home.

Everywhere we go, there are people all around us.

The fields are ripe.

How many people have I passed in my life that I completely ignored? The number is too large to bear.

It's time to open our eyes and look. The harvest is ripe all around us, and has been our entire life.

Don't let the field that God entrusted to you fall back into the ground and die.

Work the fields and reap a harvest that will never decay.

The God of Paradox

The scripture is filled with truths that appear to be paradoxical on the surface. Here are some examples:

To live, you must die.

Salvation is through faith alone, but faith without works is dead.

The first shall be last.

Man has free will, but God is controlling all things.

Jesus was fully God and fully man.

Our strength comes through weakness.

Exaltation comes through humility.

We are free by being a slave to God.

We are sinners, but God sees us as righteous (through His Son).

We are worthless servants, but we are His workmanship.

Blessed are those that hunger, but no one who comes to Him will ever be hungry.

His yoke is easy and His burden is light, but how difficult is the road that leads to life.

The Father judges impartially according to everyone's work, but the Father has given all judgment to the Son.

Let your light shine before men so that they may see your good works, but be careful not to practice your good works in front of others (don't let your left hand know what your right hand is doing).

Jesus is called the "Prince of Peace" , but He also said, "Don't assume that I came to bring peace."

We are told not to judge, but we are also told to judge according to righteous judgement.

Jesus states that He did not come to judge the world, but He also states that He came into this world for judgement.

There are many others. These truths seem to contradict one another.

At first glance to the casual observer, this might seem to disqualify Christianity as truth. That would be a hasty conclusion, especially when considering the nature of the laws that govern our existence: the laws of quantum physics.

You see, the laws of quantum physics reveal a world where paradox is the defining characteristic of all time, space, energy and matter. The quantum world exists in a state of constant and pervasive contradiction.

In quantum physics, it is quite possible for a particle to exist in a state of spinning in a clockwise direction while simultaneously spinning in a counter clockwise direction.

A particle can be in two different locations simultaneously.

A particle can exist in two different energy states simultaneously.

A particle can interfere with itself and cause itself to disappear.

In fact, the laws of quantum physics led Schrödinger to create a thought experiment that demonstrated that a cat could be both alive and dead simultaneously. (Schrödinger's Cat)

In fact, this ability of the quantum realm to exist simultaneously in mutually exclusive, paradoxical states is what gives rise to the power of quantum computers, where a Q-bit can exist in a state of being on and off at the same time.

Therefore, we see that the very substrate upon which the entire universe lives is inherently paradoxical. In fact, paradox is the very hallmark of the rules that control our existence.

If we start with the assumption that God created the universe in such a way as to parallel spiritual truths, then it makes sense that the spiritual world and the physical world are governed by paradox. In other words, if the physical universe is a physical metaphor of sorts for the rules that govern the spiritual realm, then it's no surprise that both are riddled with the incomprehensible tension of paradox.

To me, this elevates the confidence in truth of the scripture to a new realm. Instead of viewing the apparent paradoxes presented by the teaching of scripture as evidence for its inaccuracy, we should instead see this as compelling evidence that the same God who designed the functioning of the universe is the same God who created the words of scripture.

It would be a fool's errand to go about inventing a false scripture where the premise is paradox, because it would be painfully obvious to the writer that such a methodology would result in the loss of authority of the scripture due to the inherent contradictions.

Any thinking person would construct a scripture where everything agreed on the surface perfectly. Who in their right mind would embed the narrative with *apparent* contradictions that would cause it to lose credibility and believability? And how would multiple writers spanning over thousands of years all agree to such a doomed approach? The truths of quantum physics weren't known at this time.

Fast forward to the modern day where we have only unravelled the paradoxical nature of the universe in the last 100 years. To say that no one expected that quantum world to function by these rules would be an understatement. Einstein rejected quantum physics outright because he couldn't accept its ludicrous terms. Physicists are still baffled by it, and are hopelessly trying to explain what it means philosophically.

These truths presented in scripture are not contradictions. A paradox and a contradiction are two different things entirely. A paradox only appears to be contradictory until our understanding is enlightened.

I don't claim to understand all of the paradoxes presented in Scripture, but I think we can learn some profound truths:

The same paradoxical God who created the universe is the same paradoxical God who is the subject of scripture.

And this same God wants us to know something.

He wants us to know that the first will be last.

He wants us to know that to be lifted up we must humble ourselves.

He wants us to know that even though we are sinners, we are completely pure in His sight.

And He wants us to know that to live we must die.

The Body of Christ

I love the imagery that we are the body of Christ.

When you think about the crucifixion of Jesus, you realize that every part of His physical body was damaged.

His head.
His back.
His arms.
His wrists.
His legs.
His ankles.
His side.

His entire body from head to toe was hurt.

Since we are the body of Christ, this means we are each represented by different parts of His body.

Some people are the hands.
Some people are the feet.
Some people are the legs......so on and so forth.

Since Jesus' entire body was affected, this means that Jesus took the punishment for the sins of every single person.
Nobody was left out.

And every single cell in His entire body was given new life as He was resurrected.

This means that every single one of us will be resurrected.

Nobody in Christ will be left out.

We are the body of Christ, and His body was sacrificed for all of us.

The Good News and The Bad News

The good news is only as good as the bad news is bad.

If we undermine or gloss over the seriousness of sin and its consequences, then we've effectively made the bad less bad, and the good news is no longer good news.

If people don't fully understand the power of sin, then they don't fully understand the power of the gospel.

The death of Jesus on the cross makes less sense the further you gloss over sin.

And the good news loses its power.

What is there to be happy about if nothing was ever lost to begin with?

The good news is only good because there is bad news that the good news is delivering us from.

And the good news of the gospel is not that we can try really hard to be "good" by refraining from being "bad."

Human definitions of "good" and "bad" are misleading, with both being deadly.

"Good" has the power to fool people into believing they are on the road to heaven.

"Bad" has the power to fool people into believing they are unforgivable.

The gospel destroys both.

People can never be good enough to work themselves to heaven, and they can never be bad enough to preclude themselves from being forgiven.

The good news of the gospel is that good (Jesus) became bad (sin) so that the bad (us) can become good.

The Grace of Time

God surely had already imparted unto us His grace and mercy when He confined us to the dimension of time. You see, the passage of time presents each one of us with an untold number of opportunities for a fresh start, and to be forgiven of our past.

Each passing second granted to us is a new start and can stand on its own, without encumbrances from the past or worry regarding the future limiting our ability to live in the present moment of newness and forgiveness that flows eternally through Christ.

Is the guilt of your past weighing you down?

Are your mistakes too much to bear?

They need not be.

All can be made new through Christ in this present moment.

Time is a continual fountain through which the source of grace flows, not a limitation meant to confine us.

The Great Abandonment

Even if every creature under heaven stopped in their tracks this very moment and worshipped God with everything they had, this would be an infinitesimal fraction of the worship God deserves.

The true God has never been a God who said, "This is what I deserve, I demand that you give your life to me!"

Rather, the true God says, "This is what you don't deserve; I'm giving my life for you."

If you look at everything God has done and continues to do, it's all about abandoning His rights, and transferring them to us.

His entire Being is about giving rather than receiving.

God lures with love rather than forces with ultimatums.
God gives rather than takes.
God asks rather than demands.
God doesn't command worship; He loves us with such intensity that it compels us to worship.

If anyone ever had the power and the right to be a tyrannical dictator, it would be God.

Even so, He is the one who kneels down to wash dirty feet, and who willingly takes our sin, pain, shame, and suffering in His own body.

God abandoned all of His rights so that He could gain the love of a lifetime.

If God abandoned His rights, how much more should we, His creatures, abandon ours?

God taught us by example that true love can only be experienced between two individuals when they abandon their rights.

He took the first step and laid it all on the line.

Have you?

Love vs. Power

What should impress us more than anything about God is that He went to much greater lengths to prove His love for us than He did to prove His brilliance and power.

God isn't impressed with His power, nor does He have a desire to impress us with it. If He did, you would be taken on a carpet ride every day and shown infinite miracles until your heart was content.

To God, creating a vast universe with trillions of galaxies is child's play. God hasn't even come close to exhausting His creative power to impress us; for He could perform an infinite number of wonders with each wonder outdoing the previous. He could create a trillion more universes, each one more grandiose than the previous, and let you participate as an awe-struck observer. This has little value to Him. He doesn't want our attention focused on the physical.

God is more concerned about impressing you with His everlasting love.

Even though miracles are easy for Him, sacrificial love is not. God hasn't exhausted His power to perform miracles, but He has given all that He has to demonstrate His love for us. He gave His prized possession - His one and only Son. There is nothing greater God can do to demonstrate His love for us.

The fact that God hasn't taken full advantage of His power to impress or control us, and has done everything within His power to demonstrate His love for us, should tell us something very profound: God is more interested in demonstrating His love for us than He is in impressing us or exerting His power over us.

God favors Love over Power - infinitely so.
And if God favors Love over Power, so should we.

Do we try to control people with power, our talents, or our wealth? Do we use guilt, shame, or our influence to manipulate people?
God took each one these tools to control people completely off the table when He gave His one and only Son. God compels us to come to Him by showering us with the pinnacle of overwhelming love.

God chooses not to use force or coercion, and He doesn't attempt to manipulate us or impress us with miracles. God lets His love do all the talking.

And love is hard— much harder than using force or performing wonders that defy the laws of physics. Love causes pain, and it operates in the midst of enemies who spit in its face. Between the two options at God's disposal, love is the much harder of the two.

But God chose the hard path because He knew the prize - our hearts - was well worth the trip. If God chose the easy path, He would have won over our mind, not our heart. God wanted our heart, and this would not be obtained superficially or easily.

And if God, who holds infinite power in His hand, chose to lay down His ability to control us with His power, then we, who hold very little power, should follow suit.

Our greatest and only weapon should be love.

"But God demonstrates his own love for us in this: While we were still sinners, Christ died for us." - Romans 5:8

"Who, being in very nature God, did not consider equality with God something to be used to his own advantage;" - Philippians 2:6

Infinitely Away from Infinity

Each day that I become closer to God, my eyes are opened to realizing how far I was from God the day before.

I find that this process repeats ad infinitum. Even though I can become closer to God, in a very real sense I'm no closer than I was before. This is a paradox.

This experience reveals to me that there is a gap between God and us that is infinite. And it is the nature of infinite things to have this same paradox: The number 200 is closer to infinity than the number 7, but both numbers are equally infinitely away from infinity.

When the number 200 looks back into the past, he has something to boast about when he sees the number 7. When he looks forward, he has nothing to boast about. The only problem is that the number 200 has no understanding of infinity, and so looking forward becomes an impossible task for him. He doesn't realize where he is in the grand scheme of things.

But one day, the number 200 will transform into the number 300 and he will realize that 200 wasn't as great as he thought. And if he starts to catch on to this pattern as it repeats, he might be able to surmise that he is infinitely away from something that is fundamentally unobtainable. In a very small but very impactful way, he begins to appreciate the paradox of infinity.

Then comes the grand revelation: He needs someone or something to close this infinite gap. He's never going to get there on his own.

A gap is always between two ends. On one end is infinity. On the other end is the finite. He needs someone that is both infinite and finite to connect both ends of the gap.

Since he, a man, is on one end, and God is on the other, he needs someone who is both God and man to connect this infinite divide.

He needs the infinite and the finite dwelling together.

He needs God in the flesh.

"For there is one God, and there is one mediator between God and men, the man Christ Jesus." - I Timothy 2:5

"Who, though he was in the form of God, did not count equality with God a thing to be grasped, but made himself nothing, taking the form of a servant, being born in the likeness of men." - Philippians 2:6-7

"For in him the whole fullness of deity dwells bodily," - Colossians 2:9

Faith and Science

Can faith and science coexist?

This is a question that many people struggle with.

Unfortunately, this is the wrong question. People aren't asking the right question.

The question should be, "Can science tell us *everything* there is to know about existence?"

If the answer to that question is yes, then there is no need for faith. If the answer to that question is no, then faith is necessary to complete our picture of the world in which we live.

If we claim the answer to that question is yes, then we are stating that everything is measurable. But, a problem arises when we ask the next logical question, which is: "How do we know that everything is measurable?"

When we try to answer that question, the only response we can provide is, "Well, we know everything is measurable because everything science has learned thus far has been measured."

This, of course, is circular reasoning.

So, science can't tell us if everything in existence can be measured, because the only things that science can tell us about are things that can be measured. By definition, science can't tell us about immeasurable things. Science is based on measurement. If there are things out there in existence that can't be measured, we'll never be able to measure them.

So, where does that leave us? It leaves us here: Science can't answer the question, "Can science tell us *everything* about existence?" Science, by definition, is not capable of providing an answer to this question. Science can only tell us about things that science can tell us about.

And if we can't use science to answer that question, then faith is the only thing left that can.

So, faith and science are needed to form a complete picture of existence. One tells us about things that are measurable, and the other tells about things that are not.

The Bible expresses is this way:

"Faith is the substance of things hoped for, the evidence of things not seen." - Hebrews 11:1

I believe the conundrum we are faced with when we ask the question, "Can science and faith coexist?", is premised on the faulty logic that somehow science is equipped to answer all of our questions. We've placed science on a throne it doesn't deserve.

By believing that science has unbounded capabilities to provide answers about any question asked of it, we have effectively precluded any option of considering faith because faith doesn't add anything to the discussion if science is capable of accessing all knowledge.

However, if we place science back in its proper position by recognizing its limitations and inability to address the immeasurable, faith is afforded a place at the table. And when faith takes its place at the table, there is no conflict, and science will not ask him to leave.

When we allow science and faith to work together, we benefit immensely, because we have now opened up our ability to know both the measurable and the immeasurable.

If Only

"If only God would create something from nothing, then I would believe in God."

God: I already did that when I created the universe and everything in it.

"If only God would create a person out of thin air, then I would believe in God."

God: I already did that when I created Adam and Eve.

"If only God would heal someone where it was obvious there were no other explanation, then I would believe in God."

God: I already did that...countless times, and I continue to do that.

"If only God would do a miracle in my life, then I would believe in God."

God: "I already do that, every second of every day. I continually uphold every law that allows the complex machine of your body to live and breathe. This is a continual miracle."

"If only God would come down to earth and talk to me on my level, then I would believe in God."

God: I already did that when I came as Jesus.

"If only God would record everything He did and talk to me personally in a letter, then I would believe in God"

God: I already did that when I wrote the Bible.

"If only God would raise someone from the dead, then I would believe in God."

God: I already did that, many times, including my Son, Jesus.

"If only God would show me that He really loves me, then I would believe in God."

God: "I already did that, when I died for your sins."

"If only God would talk to me right now, then I would believe in God."

God: You can talk to me right now, or anytime you want. Just pray and I will answer.

The Relentlessness of the Flesh

Our flesh will do anything to find or make up excuses to prevent us from being close to God.

It will create temptations.
It will create busy work.
It will create goals and tasks.
It will create visions of grandeur that enrapture our soul to what this world has to offer.
It will create distraction after distraction, excuse after excuse.

The flesh will literally do anything within its power to keep us from becoming closer to God.

The flesh will even create fake substitutes to stand in the place of God. Paper tigers, idols, and replacements. These are decoys that trick us into thinking we're following God, so we'll stop the real pursuit.

Our spirit is willing, but our flesh is weak.

And our flesh is at war with God.

To misdirect our attention elsewhere, our flesh creates replacements to satisfy our spirit's desire to know God.

Our spirit wants to be close to God, so our flesh creates other things to be close to.
Our spirit wants to worship God, so our flesh creates other things for us to worship.
Our spirit wants to spend time with God, so our flesh creates other things to take up our time.
Our spirit wants to love God, so our flesh creates other things for us to love.

Wherever our spirit has a desire, our flesh steps in and attempts to fulfil that desire with a cheap substitute. It does this so that our spirit will shut up.

The flesh actually believes that these cheap substitutes will satisfy our quench enough so that we aren't compelled to look for more.

Will they?

There is absolutely no substitute for God.
There is no substitute for His love.
There is no substitute for His mercy.
There is no substitute for His forgiveness.
There is no substitute for His time.
There is no substitute for His gifts.
There is no substitute for His wisdom.

Yet, our flesh stands in the gap between us and God by offering us counterfeits that are designed to satisfy us "just enough" to soothe us for a short time.

However, there is no replacement for God.

Why? Because there is only one God, and He is infinite. Where would you even go to begin to find a replacement? By definition He has no replacement.

But our flesh will try to convince us otherwise, or to make us so busy so that we don't have time to think too deeply about the fact that we're busy replacing God with other things.

Our flesh flashes flashy things in our face to divert our attention away from what we really need. Why?

Because our flesh is at war with God. There are no exceptions. This is true for everyone. It has been this way since the time you were born. And if you've already given your life to Him, your flesh is still at war with Him.

The only way to win this war is to kill our enemy. The flesh needs to die.

If there were something whose stated mission was to keep you away from God at all costs, wouldn't you want to kill that thing dead? The problem with this particular enemy is once it dies, it's not permanently dead. The flesh resurrects every single day, and needs to be put to death every single day.

The flesh isn't going away without a fight.

Remember the movie 'The Terminator'? The Terminator wouldn't stop at any cost.
Your flesh is the Terminator.
It won't stop.
Ever.
Since it will never stop, you can't let your guard down.
Ever.

How do you kill the flesh?
By choosing to walk in the Spirit.
It sounds easy, but it's certainly anything but.
The flesh is a fearless and relentless opponent.

"So I say, walk by the Spirit, and you will not gratify the desires of the flesh. For the flesh desires what is contrary to the Spirit, and the Spirit what is contrary to the flesh. They are in conflict with each other," - Galatians 5:16-17

Listen to God's Spirit.

Walk constantly in the Spirit, and you will realize when the flesh is attempting to distract your attention away with something else.

And when the flesh comes in hand with this temptation, asking you to replace God with something else you can politely say, "No thank you" and continue your walk with the Spirit.

You get to choose.
Choose the Spirit.
There is no replacement for God.
Always remember that, because your flesh wants you to forget that.

Living While Dead

Is the purpose of your life to ensure that you make it to your death in one piece?

Are you just living out your days impending until you die?

Biding your time?

Are you on autopilot, day in and day out, going through the same motions until life is no more?

If you're just living to die, then you're already dead.

When we try like the dickens to save our life at the expense of not living our life, we are just as good as dead.

God wants to do so much through us, but He can't accomplish a single thing through our life if we're already dead.

Live your life like you're alive, and God will use you.

Even God Walked by Faith

Even though He is the all-knowing, all-powerful One, who holds all past, present and future in His hand, He did not allow Himself to escape the process of living by faith.

In Jesus, He emptied Himself of knowledge and power and learned to walk every second by complete faith. The One who had no need for faith saw fit to put Himself in a position where He was required to live by faith, and in the process demonstrated to us by example that we should live the same way.

For if even God, who had no need for faith lived by faith, how much more should we who do have a need for faith live by it?

For the Greater Good

The human body has two types of systems: systems that build things to make things go right, and systems that repair things when things go wrong.

DNA is constantly under attack by oxidants and mutagens. Cells are endowed with a sophisticated army of nano-sized repair machines that look for damage and repair the DNA back to its original state.

However, sometimes the repair systems are overwhelmed and some damage is not repaired.

If enough damage accumulates in the genetic instructions, that cell can become a danger to the rest of the organism. It can become cancerous and spread throughout the body.

Just like sin.

As another layer of protection, the cells have another system that monitors the overall health of the cell. If the cell senses that it has accumulated too much damage, and is now a danger to the organism, it will begin a process of self-destruction called "apoptosis". Apoptosis is programmed cell death.

The cell will execute a long series of programmed events to systematically take itself out of commission. The cell will dismantle itself, step by step, piece by piece. It dismantles itself in such a way so that the pieces are reusable by the other cells.

The cell goes through this process for the greater good. It realizes that its death will save the organism, and that the life of the organism is more important than its own.

This process reminds me of someone else who sacrificed His Life for the greater good. This person took on our damage and underwent apoptosis to save the rest of the organism.

And every step leading up to His death was perfectly programmed and executed according to a master plan.

Christ asked that this cup be taken away if at all possible. But He realized His death was necessary for the good of all humanity.

He also realized that His death was necessary for the good of you.

The Only Way

Something a pastor mentioned in one of his sermons really hit me: if Jesus is just one of many different ways to God, then certainly God was profoundly cruel by having his one and only Son die in the way that He did.

If there are many ways to God, then throwing your Son into the mix by humiliation and painful death was completely unnecessary and heartless. It would have been more merciful to just allow the other countless ways to serve as the pathway. What more was gained by sending your Son to such a fate?

Nothing.

Therefore, since Jesus died, this is proof that He is the only way. It's self-evident that God would only allow such a solution to man's malady if it were the only way. The death of Jesus and the unitary solution of the gospel go hand in hand; they are flip sides of the same coin.

Those who want to make Jesus equivalent to one of many options fashion God into a cruel monster. Which is ironic, since the motivation of such an expansion of the gospel is normally driven by a desire to make God into a jolly old chap.

Unwittingly, they've made God even more cruel than what they have already made themselves believe. Attempting to make God more palatable to your senses only makes God even less palatable.

The only way Jesus' death makes any sense at all is if it is the only way to God.

"Jesus answered, "I am the way and the truth and the life. No one comes to the Father except through me." - John 14:6

Not Too Dumb and Not Too Smart

We find ourselves in a unique position in the universe.

Einstein once said, "As a human being, one has been endowed with just enough intelligence to be able to see clearly how utterly inadequate that intelligence is when confronted with what exists."

This statement could not be more true, and this truth is of profound importance.

If we were endowed with less intelligence, we would not have the wherewithal to appreciate the vast difference between ourselves and the infinite. Our lack of intelligence would preclude us from realizing that there is something out there much greater than us.

If we were endowed with more intelligence, we may have too strong an inclination to discount the immensity of limitlessness. Our self-prescribed pride would blind us to accepting how small we really are.

In contrast to these extremes, we've been supplied with the perfect amount of brilliance; our capacity to compare our existence with the majesty of Who created our existence is ideally balanced on a narrow apex.

On one side of this apex is blind and deaf obliviousness.

On the other side of the apex is arrogant autonomy.

It's almost as if we've been perfectly created to operate by......faith.

The Reverse Golden Rule

What would your life look like if you treated yourself the way you treat others?

We normally think of the golden rule - "treat others the way you would want to be treated" - as a call to treat people with kindness, because we wanted to be treated with kindness.

But what if we interpreted this truth as its converse?

What if we kept treating people the same, and treated ourselves exactly like we treat others right now?

What if "love thy neighbor as thyself" became "love thyself as thy neighbor"?

Would we be willing to treat ourselves the same way we do others?

Would we go without food, water, shelter, and clothing?

Would we ignore and conveniently forget about our own needs?

Would we judge ourselves with the same level of unbridled scrutiny, lack of empathy, hardness of heart, and unforgiveness?

Would we talk bad about ourselves?

Would we fail to pray for our own needs and desires?

Would we put ourselves last on our list of priorities?

The fact is, all of us do a pretty good job of making sure we are taken care of, and the recipient of grace and the benefit of the doubt. We don't even think about it - it comes naturally.

But what if we walked a mile in the shoes that we make others wear?

We're Not God

Many people render a negative opinion of God based on their limited observation over an infinitesimal slice of time. Any opinion on God that humans can conjure up is fraught with this limitation.

This is presumptuous. The amount of time we actually experience is virtually non-existent compared to an infinite timeline, yet, it is the entire timeline of events that we need to consider before we can even "pretend" to judge God.

Not only do we need access to an infinite timeline, we need access to every single event that's ever occurred across that timeline. We need infinite visibility into the facts that surround every circumstance and outcome.

Not only would we need access to the entire timeline and knowledge about every event along that timeline, we would need an infinite level of wisdom to interpret that incredible amount of information and to assess its virtue or lack thereof.

So, to form an opinion on God that even comes close to fair, we would need:

Infinite Time.
Infinite Visibility (Knowledge).
Infinite Wisdom.

Here is what we do have:

Infinitesimal Time.
Infinitesimal Visibility.
Infinitesimal Wisdom.

It turns out that there is only one person who meets those three requirements. There's only one person who is equipped with the right tools to fully understand God.

God.

And, therefore, there is only one person who has the right to judge God.

God.

Yet, humans look at one event in history, or one event that occurred in their life, and hastily form a permanent opinion about God. They judge the infinite using a finite set of tools.

Our best source to go to for an accurate assessment of God is......God, because He is the only one equipped with the right tools.

If you want to know about God, go to God.

And when you go to God, you find that there is only one event in history that you need to grasp in order to understand the goodness and the love of God. You don't need access to infinite wisdom, infinite visibility, or infinite time.

And you don't need access to infinity because God became finite. He entered our realm as one of us. God embraced human flesh and exchanged His infinity for humanity.

And then, in the ultimate expression of love, He freely and willingly laid down His life on the cross to take the punishment for my sin. And in the same moment, He would forgive those who mocked and tortured Him, even though they weren't even worthy to tie His sandle.

There's nothing else that you or I need to know in order to understand the goodness, the love, and the forgiveness of God.

If you're still attempting to form your opinion of God by studying the circumstances of the world around you, with the limited brain, limited visibility, and limited time that you possess, then I ask you this question: how can you be confident that your assessment is fair, or even correct in the smallest amount?

A while back, I went through a phase where I thought I could do just this. And it was the most miserable period of my life, to the point where I came dangerously close to becoming an atheist. I don't talk about this time, or even like to think about it very much, but thanks be to God because He just laughed at me and then saw fit to open my eyes and draw me back to Him.

If you now find yourself in a similar phase of questioning God's goodness, my prayer for you is that you would put down your meager weapons and that you would quickly realize, like I, that you utterly lack the tools to judge God.

I've found that the only thing worth focusing my finite mind on is just how much God infinitely loves me.

A Razor's Edge

I find it really interesting that God created us and our surroundings in such a way that death is just a heartbeat away in any direction. We are literally living while balanced on a razor's edge.

He could have created us and our encompassing world such that the prospects of surviving were not so precarious, but He obviously did it this way for a very important reason.

Here are some examples to make it more clear:

Our bodies require a continual supply of oxygen. If this oxygen supply is removed for even a few minutes, we're dead. We're always a few breaths away from death.

If the pressure of the air is too high or too low, we're dead.

Our bodies require a continual supply of water. A few days without water and we're dead.

Our bodies require a continual supply of food. A month without food and we're dead.

The earth is surrounded by the cold vacuum of space. If we venture off the earth even a hair's width into the vastness of space, we're toast.

We would die from the lack of oxygen, the low pressure, the low temperature, and cosmic radiation.

If our bodies get too hot or too cold, we're toast.

Our bodies are immersed in trillions upon trillions of microscopic pathogens that stand at the door ready to gain a foothold and kill us.

The telomeres of our DNA continually shorten after each cell division cycle, and when they reach the end of their useful life, we die.

When DNA is copied during each cell cycle, mutations are naturally introduced due to the inherent error rate of the copying enzymes. If left unchecked, we would all die of cancer quickly after we exited the womb, if we made it that far.

When we're born as new-born babies, we're completely dependent on someone else to take care of us or we die.

And the list goes on and on.

God's creation is filled with multiple layers and sources of impending death. But, in every instance of mortal danger staring at us in the face, God provides a solution that perpetually keeps us alive.

God created plants that fill the planet and which produce a continual source of oxygen. He created the sun to provide continual energy to those plants and to warm our atmosphere.

God created the amount of atmosphere and the gravitational force of the planet such that the air pressure is just right.

God filled the earth with water and a natural cyclic filtration system that constantly replenishes clean water.

God created sophisticated temperature control systems in our body to keep our body temperature regulated.

God created the food cycle, which starts with the sun, which powers food synthesis of plants, which then serves as a perpetual source of food for all animals.

God created an atmosphere, a magnetic field, and a gravitational field that continually protects us from the deadly conditions of space.

God created a multilayered immune system comprised of millions of different nano-components which defend our bodies continually from pathogens.

God created the enzyme telomerase which restores the length of our telomeres.

God created 130 different DNA repair enzymes that continually scan the DNA for damage in each one of our cells and repair the damage within minutes.

God provides us with parents who take care of us so that we don't die.

For every pathway to instant death, God has provided us with a perfect companion that keeps us alive. This perfect balance maintains our life, and if any one of these balancing forces were removed, we would die in a very short period of time.

So, why didn't God just create us and world such that we would just survive? He could have created a person that didn't need air, food, water, perfect temperature, gravity, magnetic fields, telomerase, DNA repair enzymes, an immune system, parents, and the countless other things we need to live second by second.

I believe in choosing to create us in this way, God is trying to communicate to us a very important lesson, and the lesson is this:

God wants us to know that He is our constant sustainer and provider.

He is our second-by-second manna.

God surrounds us with death on all sides, and then He provides a constant barrier that protects us from that deathly threat, and this protective barrier must always be maintained. He is teaching us that we can trust Him all of the time. He is teaching us to rely on Him constantly.

He is our Defender.
He is our Provider.
He is our Protector.
He is our Life Sustainer.

He is teaching us that there is never a single moment that we don't need Him.

Going To War

Motives are sneaky rascals.

They have the uncanny ability to surreptitiously slip under the radar for an indefinite period of time, unless we are vigilant and consciously go on a seek and destroy mission.

Motives live at the very base layer of our mind, and all thoughts and actions project outward from this root. The problem we are faced with is the fact that motives don't want us to be consciously aware of their identity or true form. So, they build a hedge of protection around them; a series of moats and defensive boundary layers that shield their presence from our immediate senses. Motives have multiple ways to wall themselves off from our awareness.

It's in their best interest to hide. They're smart and they're fully aware that they lack any form of true virtue. They realize their self-serving nature, and if they're found out for who they really are, we'll replace them with more virtuous ones. They don't want to upset the apple cart. Motives are street smart— they've learned how to survive. They've found out the best way to survive is to bury themselves deep within our subconscious and hide.

To continue their masquerade, they've come up with innovative ways to keep us in the dark regarding their presence. One very effective tactic that motives use is to create decoys. These decoys are branded with the label "our true motives" and then they are floated up to our conscience to convince us that they are our authentic motives. These decoys are impostors. When we take the first step in checking our motives, it is these decoys that we find. They look virtuous. We're satisfied with what we find, and we continue down our path without looking deeper.

Our true motives laugh, because most of us don't think to go deeper. We're naive. We don't have any reason to find out if these decoys are real or not.

Our true motives know that we won't take the next step. Why? Because they know we truly desire what they (our true motives) are compelling us to pursue. Our flesh wants it. And when we discover that our "impostor motive" is virtuous, we are even more motivated to pursue its desires because we are now able to rationalize that our pursuit is noble. We are self-deluded and have both unwittingly and wittingly buried our heads in the proverbial sand, convincing ourselves that the decoys are the real deal.

Realize the predicament we are now in. We have convinced ourselves we are pursuing something for a virtuous reason, and so we dig in deeper. We are destroying ourselves and others around us while we are under the impression that we deserve an award.

Now, if we get a little smarter and go deeper, we might not like what we find. It's tough to come to the realization that we've been operating with impure intentions, and that our core isn't who we thought it was.

Nobody wants to do the hard work to find this out. So, our true motives know that we have a built-in deterrent to go looking for them. We are much more inclined to hear the voice of the ear-tickling impostor than to hear the voice of an enemy that may put an abrupt end to our party which we are wholeheartedly enjoying.

We're more incentivized to hide our face from our true motives because deep down we are fully aware that we'll have to stop our selfish pursuit if we are consciously aware that our motives are not good. So we keep ourselves from really trying to discover our true motive.

I've been trying to do this hard work. It's a daily battle. As I go deeper, they launch other more confounding tactics to obfuscate their existence. I've found that they have a line of defenses that I haven't even begun to fathom.

This, my friends, is what the Bible is referring to when it's talking about our "flesh."

And this is why the Bible tells us that our heart is deceptive.

Only God can probe and uncover its hidden depths. Only God can cut out our heart and give us a new one.

We must die. But, to die we have to identify our true nature. We have to stop pretending these hidden motives don't exist, or that they have somehow disappeared.

Our motives have dug themselves in and have drawn the battle lines.

And they have mounted layers upon layers of defenses.

Will you go to war?

The Son and the Sun

While driving her to school one morning, my little girl said, "Hey look!!! The sun is following us, Dad!"

I replied, "Really?? Wait, you mean us???!!

You're right! It is following us.
Let's see if it stops when I stop at the stop light.
Look!! It stopped!
Let's see if it starts following us again when I start moving.
Look! It started following us again.
I wonder why it chose to follow us this morning and no one else?"

My little girl said, "We must be special!!! Like, My Little Pony special!!"

I said, "Yes, we must be special. Let's see if it follows us all the way to school."

And guess what?
It did.

When we pulled in the parking lot, it stopped at the precise moment we stopped and hovered in the sky looking directly at us.

Out of everything else that we passed that day, the sun was the only thing that followed us every step of the way and waited on us at our final destination.

But you know what?

The sun also followed every one of the 7 billion people on the planet that day.
It walked where they walked.
Stopped when they stopped.
Turned left when they turned left, turned right when they turned right, and it arrived at their destination and waited on them.

It made them feel like they were the only person on the planet. I wonder if anyone looked up that day and noticed?

Even though the sun never really moved a single centimeter, because it is always the same- it found a way to follow 7 billion people personally in an almost infinite number of different directions at the same time.

Just like the "Son" does for each one of us.

Jesus will never forsake us or leave us, and He is with us wherever we go, even though He is immovable.

The Grace of God

We're floating on a speck stranded out in the desert of space, surrounded by trillions upon trillions of miles of bone-chilling darkness; hovering here in the infinite realm where the vacuum of death rules on every side.
Yet, all 7 billion of us even tinier specks have managed to survive.

We've devised enough thermonuclear weapons to blow this speck and all the specks that live on it to smithereens multiple times.
Yet, all 7 billion of us have managed to survive.

We've replaced our food supply with toxic waste and artificial poison disguised as nutrition.
Yet, all 7 billion of us have managed to survive.

We've immersed our bodies in a constant flood of electromagnetic radiation.
Yet, all 7 billion of us have managed to survive.

Since the time we were born, we've filled our minds with violence and death.
Yet, all 7 billion of us have managed to survive.

We've created a society that glamorizes wealth, compelling us all to become slaves to incessant work and debt.
Yet, all 7 billion of us have managed to survive.

We've fanned the flames of hatred, and allowed mass genocide to exist.
Yet, all 7 billion of us have managed to survive.

And now, after floating on this speck in the vacuum of space for thousands of years we ask ourselves:
How much longer can all of us manage to survive?

The same way we've always survived.

Only by the love, patience, and grace of God.

Spiritual vs. the Physical

One of our major problems is that we don't want to go through the time or pain it takes to build the future spiritual kingdom, so we've taken it upon ourselves to build a counterfeit kingdom in the physical realm now.

The spiritual kingdom doesn't appeal to our unquenchable desire for immediacy because we believe the work is too hard, and the payoff is too far off into the future. We'd rather take matters into our own hands by controlling and manipulating this physical world into submission to create our own kingdom right now.

The physical is visible.
It's shiny.
It's colorful.
It's tangible.
It fills all of our senses with immediate sensations that scream for our attention.

We are constantly immersed in full-color 3-dimensional imagery, sounds, tastes, smells and feelings. So, we pay more attention to it and believe it's the most real thing around us.

Due to its overwhelming presence and our infatuation with it, we fool ourselves into thinking this physical reality is the *only* thing.

But the spiritual is hidden.
It takes a certain pair of eyes to see it.
It takes a certain pair of ears to hear it.
It takes a certain heart to feel it.
It takes certain mind to think upon it.

We have to tune out this physical world and quiet down. That sounds easy, but it's actually very difficult. It's something that you have to work at. You don't have to work at being enamoured with the physical; you're already hardwired to do so, and it's screaming at you for attention. Due to the immediate pleasure it promises, our mind and body are more than happy and willing to give the physical world the attention it convinced us it deserves.

But, contrary to popular belief, the spiritual world is not off in the celestial future. It's here right now. All around us. If we are in Christ, then it is already in us.

We should be building the eternal spiritual kingdom now.

Yes, it will become more "real" to us in the future, but only because the volume of the physical world will be turned down to zero and the spiritual will be the only thing left. At that time, it will immediately fill our senses like the physical world does now. It will be like changing the channel on the TV. For now, both stations are playing simultaneously, but we can only see one at a time. Just because one station is blaring at us, that doesn't mean we should give it all of our attention while neglecting the other.

Turn the dial.

We have become too impatient with the spiritual kingdom, and enamoured by the physical. So, we've let this physical world take the spiritual's place. We spend our focus, attention, time, effort, money and passion building this physical world to fall in line with our desires. This comes at the cost of abandoning the spiritual. It is left to die.

We shouldn't deny this physical world, either. We can't go on top of a mountain and pray until we die.

So, what are we to do?

Our mission should be to use the resources that we've been given in this physical world as a tool for helping us to build the spiritual kingdom.

Everything around us can be used in this way if you think about it.

That water from the stream can be put into a glass that we make from sand to give to someone who is thirsty.
That cotton growing in the field can be spun into clothing to give to the naked.
The orbit of the moon can be used to show someone that there is rhyme and reason to the universe, and that there is a God who is the "rule maker".
That phone can be used to spread the gospel across the world in a microsecond.

Everything around us that seems finite and temporal can be transformed into the eternal by repurposing it intentionally.

We need to be reminded daily to retune our glasses to see the spiritual kingdom. It's easy to fall back into the allure of the physical, and to live our lives for the physical's sake. After all, right now it's the loudest and brightest thing smacking us in the face. We have to work really hard at seeing beyond its beguile.

Do the hard work. Find creative ways that you can use this physical world to build the eternal. Take an inventory of every resource you've been entrusted with, from the biggest to the very smallest, and find ways you can use it to walk others into the spiritual kingdom.

And sit in the quiet, close your eyes, tune out this world, and talk to God. And do it often.

This is why you are on this planet right now.

This is why you have been given what you've been given.

When you make this shift in perspective and motivation, everything changes.

Why Do We Need Faith?

Are there things that God knows that we don't know, or that we can't know?

First, let's consider that God is infinite and we are finite. So, the answer to that question is a resounding yes.

It doesn't matter how many questions we ask, how deep we dig, or how hard we listen. God may choose to reveal more of Himself to us, but there will always be something that God knows that we don't know. This is true by definition because He is infinite, and we are not.

If there is always something that we don't know, will we have all of our questions answered?

No.

That being the case, it's very obvious that we need to operate by faith.

When we reject the notion that we must operate by faith, we are essentially saying that we are not satisfied existing as a finite being; that we, in fact, desire to have infinite understanding.

By refusing to operate by faith, then, we are essentially claiming that we want to be equivalent to God.

God is pleased when we operate by faith because we are acknowledging that He is God and we are not. We are confessing to Him that we are satisfied with how He chose to create us.

Operating by faith is our admission to what is already true. Whether we choose to operate by faith or not, God will always be infinite and we will always be finite. This difference is always true whether we want it to be or not.

Faith is our acquiescence and submission to the truth. Operating by faith is just our willingness to gladly accept this truth.

When you think about it, faith is the most logical position to take.

The more I learn, the more I realize that I know nothing. We have this tendency to think that we would grow more confident in our knowledge the more we learn, but it's quite the opposite. I've found that as my mind is exposed to more knowledge, I become less confident in knowledge, because each bit of new information exposes a greater measure of the unknown.

Every element of new information comes packaged with ten new questions that I didn't know to ask. So, the more I've learned, the more I've found myself having to rely on faith. We're fooled into thinking that faith is the currency of simpletons. Rather, faith is the response of someone who is wise enough to realize what they can't know.

And God is pleased when we live by faith.

"And without faith it is impossible to please God, because anyone who comes to him must believe that he exists and that he rewards those who earnestly seek him." – Hebrews 11:6

The Mirror

Could it be that the people who make us angry are simply mirrors who reflect back our own flaws? Are we angry because of seeing something in us that we subconsciously don't like? Have we projected ourselves onto them, and then misattributed their error with our own?

If that's true, think about how freeing that could be. That may be the greatest tool in our toolchest - a tool that's rusted, sitting in a hidden drawer.

It's extremely difficult to analyze ourselves, because we're helpless victims of internal-perspective blindness. Our real nature and motivations are obscured from our immediate senses. This is why the phrase, "the pot calling the kettle black" continues to live on in infamy.

But what if a mirror existed that when looked upon would reveal to us every flaw we couldn't possibly see otherwise - a mirror that provided us with an external view. And what if that mirror was accessible to us simply by studying those people that cause us to react negatively? If we discover what it is about them that we don't like, then perhaps the natural corollary is some defect in us.

And if that's true, it may be that this caustic social environment we now find ourselves immersed in may be our biggest opportunity to learn something profoundly imperceptible about ourselves.

What is it that's pushing our buttons?
What's stinging our nerves?

The important thing to realize is that it's *our* nerves that are getting stung, not the other person's.

We should always ask ourselves the next obvious question- why is this action or behavior bothering me? What's truly motivating my aversion?

It helped me to sit down and really think about specific examples of people or situations that produced negative feelings in me. Then I started peeling back the layers to find what really motivated my emotional reaction. It turned out that I wasn't mad about their worldview or actions like I thought I was. I found hidden, ugly motivations lurking inside. Not that those hidden, ugly motivations negated the error of the person, of course. It just made me realize that I wasn't mad because of some virtuosity I had convinced myself ruled my views.

To go a bit deeper about how to practically apply this, first ask yourself, "Why does this annoy me?" When you reveal the first superficial answer to that question, take that answer and analyze it the same way. Ask yourself, "now, why does this ___insert answer___ bother me?" When you've answered that, repeat the process and keep moving inward towards your true motivation.

Keep peeling back the layers. Eventually you should be able to uncover the "first cause" or the true motivation operating within your BIOS that's driving the outward, superficial response. Many times, I've discovered that this motivation is not related to the person's actions. This process of digging deeper normally ends with a very selfish reason that's been eclipsed by layers upon layers of rationalization that are masquerading as virtuous.

Now, I'm not saying that the person whose actions bother you isn't wrong in their behavior. This person could be absolutely wrong, and they may have deeper issues which need to be addressed. Keep in mind that this is undoubtedly true of all of us. However, our emotional reaction may not be as virtuous as we might first think.

Going through the process of discovering why someone's actions bother us doesn't negate what needs to change in that person– it just exposes something in us that needs changing.

Give it a try. Be honest with yourself. Don't be afraid about what you may find, we all have ugliness lurking within. That ugliness can be dealt with by giving it to Christ. The real enemy is not the ugliness lurking within, it's the untold layers that block its presence from our view.

If we can't view it, it can't be dealt with. This is why Christ dealt so harshly with the Pharisees — they refused to admit that they needed to uncover these layers which occluded their true motive.

"Why do you look at the speck of sawdust in your brother's eye and pay no attention to the plank in your own eye?" - Matthew 7:3

The Great Filter

Imagine that someone has a video of your entire life. A video of everything you've ever done, for every second of every day since the time you were born.

Now imagine two people.

One person is instructed to go through that entire video and look for the worst moments of your behavior. Their mission is to find every bad thing you've ever said or done, regardless of how embarrassing or shocking it may be. In fact, the more embarrassing the better. Tiny 30 second - 1 minute snapshots of your life that paint you in the worse possible light, all strung together into one video, with no good moments allowed. They are also instructed not to include any surrounding footage that describes the background or context of why you're acting the way you are in any given scene.

Can you picture this video of your life in your mind? I can, and it's not pretty. All I can say is I would never want this video of me to see the light of day, ever.

The second person is instructed to do just the opposite. Their mission is to assemble a montage of all of your best moments- just short snippets. They are also instructed not to show the surrounding context.

Now, imagine each of those videos being shown to a separate audience. Here's the caveat- the audiences are not told that the videos were assembled by filtering only the negative or only the positive. They are only told that this is a video about your life.

What would the first audience conclude about your character from the first video? How would they react to you afterward? Would you have any chance of convincing them that that's not who you are? Would you be able to defend yourself and change their opinion? If someone else tried to recalibrate this group's opinion of you by saying, "Wait, but you didn't see the entire story; there is good in this person," would this group readily change their perception of you?

What about the second group? How would they come away perceiving you? Would you feel that they have an accurate depiction of who you are that's not overinflated and unrealistic? Is the virtuousness that they perceive in you deserved? After they've seen this video, do you think it would be difficult to convince them otherwise by saying "Wait, I have bad stuff, too, that you didn't see."? Would they respond "Yeah, but that's ok---we know that you're a generally good person and any negative is far outweighed by your fundamentally good nature"?

This is what social media does to every single one of us. We choose to paint pictures of us that may not be realistic. This is what the news does to political candidates. They filter and spit out what their audience is wanting to see for any given person.

Perhaps even more importantly, this is what we do to ourselves when we have an overinflated or too negative view of our self-worth by the constant voices we allow into our head from the past.

After people's minds are "made up" about a certain person, or about us, it's very hard to change that afterward. Depending on what initial trajectory that person is presented, they can bifurcate into one of two polar opposite ideas about that person, with very little chance of that changing afterwards.

In essence, if we live our lives filtering the world this way, every person we have ever known is nothing more than a false caricature of that person, and we are a false caricature to others.

And we can do this to ourselves. Depending on what voices are playing out in our own mind, our perception of our self may very well be a false image of who we really are. It's very difficult to change the perception we have of our own self.

But God, God Himself, knows the REAL you. And He loves you without any added pretense, and He loves you without any self-deprecation. And God knows the person you're judging through that filter you've been presented.

I think life's grandest and most difficult challenge is to come to a place where we can truly see ourselves the way God sees us —and to see others the way God sees them.

Who Do I Need to Know?

Instead of constantly asking, "What do I need to DO?", we should be asking, "Who do I need to KNOW?"

We spend most of our thoughts on concerning ourselves with actions.

What do I need to do?
What should I be doing?
What should I start doing?
What do I need to do today?
What do I need to do this week?
What do I need to do this year?
What do I need to do to do God's will?

Do, do, do, do, do.

Instead, we should be a great deal more concerned with who we need to know. Our thoughts should be consumed with this question, "How do I become closer to God today?"

How do I get to know Him more?
How do I spend time with Him?
How do I rest in His presence and talk with Him today?
Do I know God more today than I did yesterday?

If not, why? What's in the way?

Sometimes we think that doing more things will bring us closer to God.

Not true. Don't fall for this tempting trap.

God wants us to rest in the cool of the garden, and to hear His footsteps.
God wants to walk with us and to have a real conversation with us.
God wants us to want to know Him more.

That's His true desire.

God could make all the stones of the earth get up and do what He needs to get done. But a stone won't love Him back.

God wants your heart, not your muscles.

Don't get me wrong, He will put you to work as you get to know Him.

First things first, though.

First and foremost is your heart, and then the rest follows.

If Jesus, being God, needed to spend time with God, how much more so should we?

Spend time with God today before you do anything else. If you haven't yet, now is a good time.

I Really Wish My Life Was Different

"I really wish my life was different, God. Things are all messed up in my life."

God: "How about this? I'll let you choose what you want your life to look like. Tell me your perfect life, and I'll make it happen."

"Really? Wow! Cool. Ok, hmmmm, I don't know. That's a tough one. I don't know what I really want, and I would probably choose the wrong thing. I guess I would choose for Your will to be done. So, you choose and I will accept whatever you decide."

God: "You sure?"

"Yes. Your will is always the best."

God: "Ok, wonderful. I'll set that up right now. Ok. Poof! My will is now being done in your life."

"Really? Wow! Cool. Let me check this out............
Wait, I don't notice anything different. My life seems to be exactly the same."

God: "Interesting how that works, isn't it?"

True Goodness

Being a good person doesn't bring you close to God. It's the other way around: being close to God transforms you into a good person.

The story of salvation is that man cannot save himself. When we finally admit that we can't do it, God will transfer to us all of the goodness that we need.

Goodness is not manufactured by man; it is accepted from God and flows through man.

Goodness that is manufactured by man is not goodness as God defines goodness. Goodness that is manufactured by man is a statement of self-sufficiency, autonomy, pride, and ultimately, a statement that God is not needed.

If it were possible for man to save himself, do you think God would have let His Son die on the cross in the way that He did? If that were the case, He would have just told us to get our act together. The only reason God allowed this to happen was because it is impossible for man to be his own savior, and because of His great love for us.

Jesus' sacrifice wasn't a nice "add on" just in case we needed a little extra help saving ourselves.

The good news of the gospel is that we can stop the endless and pointless struggle of striving to save ourselves.

If a person chooses to decline this offer by insisting on saving themselves, they are essentially saying to God that it was absolutely unnecessary for Jesus to sacrifice His life. Essentially, all of that pain and suffering was for naught, because this person has found a way that makes His sacrifice wholly unnecessary.

This is the same mortal error demonstrated by Adam and Eve in the garden. By choosing to eat of the fruit of the Tree of the Knowledge of Good and Evil, they were choosing to save themselves by choosing to navigate Good and Evil for themselves. They believed that by having this knowledge, they could independently synthesize goodness from their own lives, while avoiding evil at every turn.

Rather than resting in the cool simplicity of the garden with God and accepting His everlasting goodness flowing through them, they chose to venture out into the dark wilderness and to labor for a goodness that God did not recognize. Because this manmade goodness was in opposition to God's goodness, He blocked the entrance with a flaming sword.

It's time for us to venture back to the garden where we will find the flaming sword replaced by a gate with Jesus standing at the entrance with open arms. And when we enter, we must hand to Jesus the uneaten remnant of the fruit we've been holding onto for dear life.

And then, and only then, can we rest with God in the garden and allow His goodness to flow through us. And it will be there where we find the second tree - The Tree of Life - from which we can freely eat.

The Sovereignty of God

The universe is the perfect marriage of chaotic unpredictability and ordered symmetry. On one hand, it is raw and untamed--on the other, it is perfectly defined with predictably repeating patterns that can be quantified by physical laws.

An unseen abstract realm bubbles and froths with whimsical lawlessness, and this dream-like world transcends into our perceptible realm with ordered precision. This is the story told by the fuzzy and random quantum world as it forms the basis for our classical physical reality, and this story is unbelievably amazing.

The physicist has learned that the quantum realm is ripe with impossible combinations of existence that are projected into our physical reality. Somehow this random chaos results in law, logic, reason, and trust-worthy conformity. Somehow, it all works, impossible as it may seem.

We trust that this works, even though we have no explanation of how this absurd transition occurs. It shouldn't work, yet, it does - and we build our worldly faith around this. A ball falls towards the earth with clock-like precision, even though the fundamental substratum running our universe says that it shouldn't. We trust this impossible predictability with our very life.

Because we can't explain it, it requires faith.

This physical world is a perfect metaphor for picturing the mystery of the sovereignty of God.

He works behind the scenes in imperceptible and undefinable ways; ways that seem randomly arbitrary and illogical. When we attempt to peer behind the veil to understand His ways, we are presented with paradox.

We throw up our hands as we realize that there is no science that can define His thoughts. Yet, as He works the mystery of His plan, it orders our realm into purposeful meaning and serendipity. Somehow, in the end, His sovereignty is ordering the entire story of man into an intricate web that's been perfectly designed before it even came into existence. Somehow, everything is working together for our good.

The same faith we must conjure to understand our physical reality is the same faith we must use to put our lives in the hands of the mysteriously sovereign God.

The Bliss of Suffering

People want bliss without suffering.

The only problem is bliss doesn't exist without suffering.

We wouldn't even know bliss was a thing unless we experienced suffering.

Bliss doesn't exist without suffering in the same way that light doesn't exist without dark, or that up doesn't exist without down, or that negative numbers don't exist without positive numbers.

Not only does suffering allow bliss to exist, it makes bliss even more blissful, for it is the release and the relief encountered at the end of a period of suffering that causes bliss to have value in the first place.

People question whether God exists because He allows suffering to exist in His universe.

I submit to you that it is because of suffering that we know that God exists.

I would question if God were real if I found myself living in a universe that didn't contain suffering, because there would be no differentiation or distinction that would serve as a beacon to separate good from evil, and without this distinction there is no rational basis to hypothesize a God of any sort.

The banality and sterility offered by inanimate naturalism would rule the day.

So the very thing atheists use to prove God doesn't exist is the very thing that actually proves that He does exist, for the atheist would be completely incapable of recognizing or defining suffering without a God to compare it to.

Although we despise suffering, it is suffering that allows delight to be delightful, and bliss to be blissful.

The True God

What kind of God would form His creation out of dirt, not knowing what it was like to live in such a shell Himself?

What kind of God would constrain His creation to a finite world limited by space, time, and physics, and never subject Himself to those same limitations?

What kind of God would ask His creation to be obedient, and never subject Himself to authority?

What kind of God would create a Universe where His creation experienced pain, suffering, anger, evil, and sorrow, and never let Himself experience such suffering?

What kind of God would allow His creation to experience death, while never experiencing death Himself?

What kind of God would ask His creation to believe in something they couldn't see, and never empty Himself of all knowledge to walk by faith?

What kind of God would ask His creation to forgive every enemy, and never allow Himself to be hurt so that He could demonstrate that same forgiveness to His enemies?

What kind of God would ask His creation to give up their entire life to follow Him, and never surrender His own?

So, I ask you – look across all the gods of the world, and find the God that has performed every single thing that He has asked of His creation.

And when you have found Him, you have found the true God.

And So It Goes

Beauty emerges
Life begets more life.
And so it goes.

From the ground springs forth flesh.
Desperate, raw and untamed.
Light of sun and wisp of air penetrate its veins.
Till beauty resounds like praises Divine.
And purity washes like refiner's fire.
Life begets more life.
And so it goes.

Till envy of Darkness
and covetousness of Death raise their sceptre to take back the ground
from which life sprung.
To destroy that which was fashioned with Divine hand,
And imagined with Holy mind.
To blot out sun's light and suffocate air's breath
Till life is no more.
Now, life begets death
And so it goes.

So Divine becomes flesh
And takes our sin on God's cursed tree
Entering death's tomb

Life arises once more
And Life begets more life
And so it goes.

Our souls desperately yearn for a day when life's great struggle is no
more.
And beauty emerges.
And Life begets more life.
And so it goes.

Unrecognized Miracles

Most miracles go unrecognized.

To presuppose that a miracle is only a "temporary suspension of the laws of nature" is a myopic definition that removes the world of its everyday wonder.

First consider that the laws of nature are a miracle, for there is no explanation as to their source without God.

Every quantum fluctuation, every electron wavefunction, every DNA replication and cell division, every flower that blooms, every neuron firing, every electrical pulse that contracts our heart, every expansion and contraction of our lungs, every rain drop, every orbit around the sun, every lightning bolt, every supernova — they are all miracles that occur daily.

Why are they miracles? Well, I can't make any of those things happen, can you?

We've become so accustomed and desensitized to our surroundings that we now fail to recognize the awe of it all.

Just because we can predict certain events in nature with some modicum of accuracy, this in no way takes away from their miraculous nature, for it is the mere presence of this predictability and beauty that is the real miracle.

Second, I would point you to God's sovereignty over it all. When you take a deep dive into this, you find that the arrangement of events in our lives and in history happen according to God's will, even in the absence of God suspending the laws of nature. How can this be?

How can a predictable set of physical laws arrange for Jesus to be crucified at the precise time in history that God ordained, when that event was the product of a long series of free-will agents, kingdoms, nations, etc., acting throughout history in the context of predictable natural laws? Somehow God uses the very laws of nature, without altering them one bit, to accomplish His will at the exact time it's appointed to happen.

I'm sure you've seen this at work in your life, haven't you?

That random person you met at the grocery store that you knew was God's handiwork.
That mate you met in the most unexpected and serendipitous way.
That child who came to you and said just the right words at the right time.
That job that came at just the right time.
That tragedy that you couldn't explain at the time it occurred, but whose purpose became wonderfully obvious later.

None of these events are the product of a temporary suspension of the laws of nature. They were arranged through the very laws of nature.

How in the world does God do that? It's like a gigantic game of chess being played in infinite dimensions.

For God to make a dead person rise from the dead seems easy to me when I consider God's power. That temporary suspension of the laws of physics doesn't make my mind explode when I try to figure out how God did it. It's easy. He just speaks it and it happens.

But for the life of me, I can't figure out how God made sure that my wife and I would someday meet, given that that event was the product of a near-infinite set of previous decisions and activities of billions of people who preceded us.

And I most certainly can't understand how God made the star appear over Bethlehem at the appointed time, as we now how evidence that this was an alignment of planets and stars that were orbiting like clockwork. He didn't suspend the laws to make a miracle happen, the miracle was being played out in the background over centuries!

And all of that perfect timing and clockwork was being synchronized and interweaved with the finicky decisions and the free will of every individual in the human race.

These types of miracles are all around us every day, and we fail to see them.

Sit back for a moment and take a deep look at your entire life.

Do you see the miracles now?

All Because of Him

There's absolutely nothing we can do apart from God.

Can we create a single atom from nothing?

Let's try something smaller.
How about a single electron?

Let's go even smaller:
How about a quark?

Do we have the power to ensure that the atoms that make up the universe and our body will continue to be held together?

Let's go bigger.
Can we ensure the sun will rise to give energy to our planet?

Can we ensure the law of gravity will remain unchanged so that the earth continues in its present orbit?

Can we make sure that the laws of biochemistry continue to operate so that our heart beats, cells divide, neurons fire, our brain works, and our lungs take in oxygen?

Can we control the flow of time so that the next second arrives just on time?

Yet, everything mentioned above is completely necessary so that we can get out of bed every morning. And after we get out of bed, we can't even accomplish a simple thing like moving our arm without every one of those things taking place.

So, what can we accomplish without God?

Absolutely nothing.

The pride and arrogance of man is ignorant foolishness. This notion that man can accomplish anything that he puts his mind to without God is fiction. People can make themselves believe that if they want to, but not a single atom vibrates without Him sanctioning it first.

Man thinks he is on the throne, and can will himself accomplishment after accomplishment by sheer determination, will, drive, persistence and motivation. He beats his chest while shouting, "Nothing is impossible for me!"

It would be good for us to exercise humility, giving thanks to God because He allowed us to exist that day. Then, after giving thanks, we should ask God what He would have us do that day. And at the end of that day, we ought to give thanks to God for each thing He enabled us to accomplish.

It's all because of Him.

Every. Single. Thing.

Love and Hate

Love and hatred are more than just opposites; they are intrinsically different.

Love self sustains itself for eternity. Hatred is temporary because it eventually destroys itself.

Hatred and entropy are cousins. Entropy is the physical principle that all things wind down and dissipate. Entropy is a destructive property that rules the physical universe.

Hatred is the spiritual corollary to entropy, as it causes disorder and destruction.

Love is self-sustaining because it is not self-serving and it seeks to build up. Love naturally perpetuates its own existence into eternity, while hatred fulfils its own destiny, which is annihilation.

The only way existence can persist forever is if love exists.

If love doesn't exist, we don't exist. And the source of that love is God. God is love.

This is why God dwells in eternity. He has no beginning, and He has no end.

If God consisted of hatred, He would have ceased existing long ago.

God is the only one that can sustain our existence, because He is the only source of love.

Love never fails.

"Love is patient, love is kind.
It does not envy, it does not boast, it is not proud.
It does not dishonor others, it is not self-seeking, it is not easily angered, it keeps no record of wrongs.
Love does not delight in evil but rejoices with the truth.
It always protects, always trusts, always hopes, always perseveres.
Love never fails." - I Corinthians 13:4-8

Faith or Evidence?

We would all love to claim that we form our belief about God by considering evidence and operating by logic and reason.

I've fooled myself into thinking this before.

But if we use a little bit of logic and reason which we seem to be so proud of, we would quickly find it's all one big facade.

Not a single person can either prove or disprove the existence of God.

For in the wildest extreme of hypotheticals, if God were to use every power at His disposal to prove His existence, we could always claim that what we just witnessed was simply a hallucination or some other sort of grand trickery.

And in the other wildest extreme, where we search the entire universe to prove God doesn't exist, we would always be left wondering if we turned over every leaf, or whether we missed Him due to our perceptual insufficiencies, or if He were merely choosing to make Himself unknown for the time at hand.

There is no imagined proof that would suffice to prove God is real, and there is no imagined proof that would suffice to prove God is not real.

This is because our mind could always find another explanation for our observations. There are no exceptions to this pesky problem.

So, whatever your view on the matter, you are operating by faith.

We are all operating by faith. Certainly logic and reason play a role in this process, but it is not the end-all-be-all that we like to think.

We like to think evidence comes first, then faith follows.

I submit to you that faith comes first, then evidence follows.

For we are all grand masters of rejecting evidence that doesn't align with our worldview, and accepting evidence that does. We measure the veracity of evidence by our presuppositions.

But, we all like to think we're a bit more savvy than that. We pretend that we're all unbiased filters of empirical data, like we're some kind of supercomputer that's processed billions of pieces of evidence and rendered a conclusion based on our superior intellect.

That's not to say that God hasn't provided us with evidence for His existence, identity, and nature. I believe He has provided us all with more than enough evidence.

But what does one do with this evidence? — that is the question.

I can show you a wealth of data that I believe any thinking person should be able to look at and become a Christian in a microsecond.

And someone else could just as easily show me volumes of data that they believe proves otherwise.

How can two people, both with thinking minds, form such opposite conclusions from the same set of data?

Faith. That's how.

Even though there's plenty of evidence, it still requires faith to recognize it as evidence.

This is a gap that can't be filled with science. All science can do is present increasing levels of evidence. It requires faith to properly filter, interpret, and draw conclusions from that evidence.

For each new scientific discovery, a person with faith can say, "Wow, look how wonderful God is!", while another person can say, "I guess we need to go back to the drawing board and rewrite the laws of physics to account for this new discovery."

Faith plays a much bigger role in our view of the universe than most people would like to admit. We want to be the master of our own destiny, and being able to claim that we are all "unbiased evidence filters" who can rightly answer the big questions surrounding our existence provides us with a big boost to our desired autonomy. So, this pathway appeals more to our flesh and ego.

Faith takes away this perceived superpower that we believe we possess, and claims that we have to couple ourselves to a higher power (God) to rightly interpret the evidence.

"Now faith is the substance of things hoped for, the evidence of things not seen." - Hebrews 11:1

Is Evil, Pain, and Suffering Necessary?

The fact that evil, pain, and suffering exists within our universe is used by some to dismiss the possibility of the existence of God. For some reason, many people start with the assumption that God's character would prevent Him from allowing evil and suffering to exist in the first place. At the very least, it is argued, God should stop evil in its tracks.

Let's perform a thought experiment to understand this argument better.

Let's say that it is frigidly cold outside, and you have no jacket. You've been suffering in the cold for over an hour, and you believe that frostbite might be setting in if you don't get into a source of warmth soon. Suddenly, someone opens their door to you and lets you into their home. The temperature is a cozy 72 degrees, and the feeling of blissful warmth overtakes your body. You tell yourself that this is the best feeling of your life.

The funny thing is, you've spent your entire life at 72 degrees, and you never realized it was warm until now. It's not until this moment of being exposed to the frigid cold that you realize for the first time how wonderful 72 degrees really is. Your body had become accustomed to 72 degrees, so much so that you were numb to its presence. YOU NEVER REALIZED THAT 72 DEGREES WAS WARM UNTIL YOU

EXPERIENCED THE FRIGID COLD. And it was at that precise moment that you learned to appreciate 72 degrees.

Now, let's say you've lived your entire life as if a bright flashlight were shining directly into your eyes. Since the day you were born, all that your visual cortex has perceived is pure white light. You haven't been able to make it go away. Because this is all you know, it never crossed your mind to make it go away. In fact, you never even knew that this was light, or that it was white. You never realized it was even there, or it was a thing. You never thought to ask, "where is this white light coming from?" because it is all you have ever experienced. To you, it's as if the light doesn't even exist! You've never experienced anything else, so you believe this is all that there is. You had no reason to call this light, or to even ponder the existence of light. If someone had come up to you and attempted to describe to you what light was, you wouldn't know what they were talking about, even though you had experienced pure white light your entire life!

Now, in contrast, in the real world, the only reason we our able to define and recognize light as a thing is because we are able to experience its absence. The contrast between its presence and absence alerts us to the fact that it exists.

These physical metaphors teach us a very important lesson: that for anything to be defined and recognizable, it needs to be compared to its absence or opposite. To us, a "thing" doesn't even exist until we can experience its absence, its opposite, or something else which is much different. There is simply no way around this.

Applying this principal to the goodness of God, we quickly see that it would be impossible for us to experience the goodness of God, or to even recognize it as a thing, until we experience its opposite. Its opposite has a name – evil. The goodness and perfection of God is like pure white light. If all we ever experienced since the moment we were born was the pure white light of God being transported to the visual cortex of our soul, we would never know that God was good. We wouldn't even know what "good" was, or that there was such a thing to be defined at all.

Just like the person who felt the blissfulness of warmth for the first time when they were no longer immersed in cold, we will experience blissful relief and overwhelming joy when we are no longer immersed in evil and are finally surrounded by His unadulterated goodness. And the light we are surrounded by will be the purest, whitest light we have ever experienced when we are no longer immersed in darkness.

Taking this thought process one step further, since God is the only real source and definition of goodness, if we were never able to define or experience goodness, then it naturally follows that we would never know who God is, or that the concept of "God" was even something to ponder.

To recognize the identify and presence of God, we need to experience His absence, and because He is the only source of goodness, we must also experience the absence of goodness.

Adam and Eve were the first people to learn this hard lesson. They partook of the Tree of the Knowledge of Good and Evil (notice the contrast), and they were immediately barred from the presence of God. It was at this time they realized that the absence of God would bring forth evil, darkness, and death.

And the rest of humanity was plunged into the darkness of sin and death. But, then the Light of the world arrived on the scene and flooded everyone's eyes with light. Jesus is the true Light, who gives light to everyone. And this light is recognizable because we were living in darkness.

This process is continued to teach us about life. Jesus had to die, so that we could live. And we, in turn, have to die before we can live. Before we can understand and appreciate true Life, we all have to go through the process of death.

God is taking us through a process, and there is a reason for the process we are going through. To accuse God of wrongdoing or to claim He doesn't exist because He allows evil to persist is a very superficial and short-sighted understanding of His ultimate work in us.

God doesn't allow anything that isn't necessary, so pain and suffering must be necessary to accomplish His ultimate plan in us.

"The people walking in darkness have seen a great light; on those living in the land of deep darkness a light has dawned." – Isaiah 9:2

Rules Can't Save You

If you want to rely on a set of rules to save you, there are two pitfalls that will trap you.

There are only two scenarios:

Scenario A: you will inevitably fail to follow this checklist of rules. If you recognize and admit this failure, this will produce shame. Shame will have the tendency to keep you from approaching God.

Scenario B: you will inevitably fail to follow this checklist of rules. If you don't recognize and admit this failure, you will be filled with undeserved arrogance and pride. Pride will keep you away from God.

This is what manmade religion results in.

Shame, or pride.

Unshakeable guilt, or self-righteousness.

The end result is the same— separation from God.

Jesus came so that we would recognize that the way to God is through faith, mercy, and grace. This will always drive us towards God, not away.

Listen to God

Your perception of you is wrong.

In the same way that you can never view yourself as you truly appear, (unless you use a mirror or camera, and this image is not the same as looking directly at you), and in the same way that it's impossible to hear what your voice really sounds like to others— it's impossible for you to truly form a correct picture of who you truly are.

You are helplessly confined by the limitations imposed by internal perspective bias, which is just a fancy way of saying that you can't truly know who you are on the inside because you're you.

Imagine the color green trying to understand, all on its own, the color green. How would green truly know the essence of green, if all green knows is green? What kind of opinion would green form of itself if it didn't have the proper perspective to understand the color green?

Well, since green can't know green, green will make up stories about itself which are nothing but a by-product of green's wild imagination, and none of these stories or opinions would be true.

Truly understanding yourself, as yourself, is as hopeless as getting inside a car and pushing on the front window from the inside to make the car move. Or as futile as trying to go to the moon by pulling up on your jeans.

What kind of wild stories have you made up about yourself? What is your opinion of you? What does your internal voice tell you on a daily basis about you?

Well, if those opinions and stories are arising in your own mind, they are all worthless because they are nothing more than your mind filling in the blanks because it doesn't have the capacity to synthesize an accurate picture of itself. It's all wild speculation that you have convinced yourself is true, and, thus, you believe it as objective fact.

So, how can you get an accurate picture of you?

To do this, you need to tap into the perspective of someone who can see you from the outside, and who has direct access to your inside. Having access to your outside from the outside is not enough, for the true you is not living on the outside - the true you is living on the inside. And no other human has access to your inside.

Therefore, you cannot trust another person to render a true picture of who you truly are, because they only see the external you. They can tell you how you appear on the outside, and they can make inferences about what you may be like on the inside based on what they see on the outside, but that's all they would ever be able to provide you- a guess.

I wouldn't base my true identity on someone else's best guess. They can't even understand themselves, let alone you.

So, if you can't rely on your view of you, and if you can't rely on someone else's view of you, where do you go to get an accurate picture of you? To do this, you need someone who has direct access to your inside from the outside, and who isn't you.

God is the only one who meets those requirements.

"The LORD does not look at the things people look at. People look at the outward appearance, but the LORD looks at the heart." - I Samuel 16:7

Since God is the creator of your soul, your heart, your mind, and everything about you, He has direct access to see you transparently from the outside all the way to the inside.

God knows more about you than you know about yourself. Not only does He know more about you, His knowledge of you is accurate, while your knowledge of you is helplessly inaccurate.

If we ever want to get out of the pointless cycle of evaluating ourselves and listening to our destructive inner voice, we need to go directly to God.

God will tell me about me.

To access that knowledge about me from God, I can do two things.

First, I can talk to Him. I can spend time with Him and directly communicate with Him. This is called prayer. As I communicate with God in a deeper and more intimate way, He will reveal to me more about me.

Second, I can read His letter to me. God's Word will tell me about me, because it's a mirror that we can look into and see ourselves.

What voices have you been listening to about you? Have you believed this voice, followed it, and conducted your life by what it tells you?

If it's not God's voice, it's wrong. By definition it's wrong, because if the voice is anything but God's voice, it doesn't possess the qualifications to form any sort of realistic picture of you.

You can't do it, so stop listening to yourself.

Someone else can't do it, so stop listening to others.

Only God can do it, so start listening to Him.

"I will listen to what God the Lord says; he promises peace to his people, his faithful servants—but let them not turn to folly." – Psalm 85:8

Imperfection

When God had finished making everything, He said that it was "good."

Notice what He didn't say. He didn't say that it was perfect.

Why didn't He make His creation, including us, perfect? Wouldn't that have been better?

Given the choice, why did He make everything imperfect?

Perhaps God reasoned He was already perfect, and He wanted His creation to be different than Him.

Perhaps God didn't want it to be easy.

Perhaps God wanted an adventure.

Perhaps God wanted someone to love, and love implicitly draws its power from the tension caused by imperfection.

Perhaps God wanted us to love Him, and if we were perfect, we could never truly love Him because it would have been our only choice.

Perhaps God wanted to demonstrate His ability to transform the imperfect into the perfect.

Perhaps God wanted to demonstrate His patience, long suffering, mercy, and forgiveness, and perfect creatures would have never given Him that opportunity.

Perhaps God wanted to know what it felt like to be hurt, to experience pain, to be rejected, and to love despite this.

A perfect universe seems good at first, but it would have lacked anything of true value. An imperfect universe gave both us and God an opportunity to experience the adventure of a lifetime.

He Chose

Whenever I'm reading through the Bible, I always dread when I start getting close to the crucifixion. I want to slow down my reading pace to delay the inevitable, or to skip over it entirely.

But then I tell myself that I must make myself read through it, as painful as it is. It's necessary for me to be reminded and to understand how much Jesus loves me, and without understanding the pain and rejection He experienced on my behalf in a very real, raw way, I'll never fully know the love of Christ. So, I push through.

It tears me in two to be reminded of Jesus' pain, suffering, and rejection. I always wonder how He felt that night in the garden when He was praying and none of His closest followers would even stay awake and pray with Him. How rejected He must have felt when all of his friends fled and denied Him, and left Him to be ridiculed, flogged and hung on a cross.

Knowing that one of His inner circle of confidants would turn Him in for 30 pieces of silver.

Knowing that even His Father would forsake Him.

The entire universe turned its back on Him.

And that also means ME. I turned my back on Him. I denied Him three times before morning, and I sold Him for 30 pieces of silver. I hammered the nails in, and I yelled "crucify Him" when given the choice to set Him free. I mocked Him and pressed the crown of thorns in.

I stood in the background with Mary and watched Him breathe His last.

Realizing this makes it even harder to read through this section.

Yet, He still demonstrated His love for all of us by CHOOSING to die for us. It was His decision. Not Pilate's. Not the Pharisees, the chief priests or the Sanhedrin. It was His own.

He chose to lay down His life.

When He dipped the bread with Judas and instructed Him to do what he must do.
When He said, "Not my will, but yours" in the garden.
When He didn't answer Pilate's questions to vindicate Himself.
When He didn't call down legions of angels to set Him free.
And when he screamed, "Into your hands I commend my Spirit."

In each one of these instances, He was making a choice to give His life away.

One thing I never caught before is Pilate's reaction to when Jesus finally passed away (recorded in Mark). He was shocked that it had happened so soon. Sometimes it would take days for someone to die from crucifixion.

So, when Jesus said, "Into your hands I commend my spirit," He was willingly giving His life away. Natural death did not overtake Him.

What does this mean?

It means He was in control the entire time.

This was His choice to follow His Father's will.

Wow.

He was led like a lamb to the slaughter, but in reality He was a lion the entire time.

And I would encourage you to read through these sections of scripture periodically. Keep it in the forefront of your mind.

We all need to be reminded of this one event that transformed all of history, and that stands at the door waiting to transform us.

"This is how we know what love is: Jesus Christ laid down his life for us. And we ought to lay down our lives for our brothers and sisters." – I John 3:16

Real Success

Have you ever put your heart and soul into something only to have it "fail"? (insert your definition of failure here).

I tend to beat myself up and have a pity party when something I spend a lot of time working on doesn't go in the direction I had hoped. I have a long list of "failures."

Maybe you do, too.

But I learned a valuable lesson. Often times, our definition of success is way off target.

To give you an example: I enjoy composing music on the piano, and I've put out several piano albums. I pretty much had chalked them up to mediocre failures because they didn't live up to my "expectations." But, it was something that I personally enjoyed doing, nonetheless.

That all changed when I received this message from a lady that totally changed my definition of success.

"Doug. I wanted to tell you how appreciative I am of your piano music during this phase of my life. I am going through a very, very hard and rough patch, leaning on God to get me through. Some days, I wish I could just leave this place I am in. But that is not going to happen.

Your music is very calming to my broken soul and spirit. I just wanted you to know."

Wow.

If this was the only positive thing that ever came out of the thousands of hours I put into piano music, it would have made it all worth it.

This should be our definition of success.

What about you? Is there something in your life —a talent, effort, or a desire —that hasn't panned out the way you wanted? Something that you quit doing because you didn't see it "succeeding"?

What if you were meant to do that thing with all of your heart and strength for just one person? Maybe it's one person that you don't even know exists and that you never get to hear from.

What if that was the definition of success? What if you were already successful at that thing you thought you had failed at, and because of a misguided definition of success, you quit?

If so, then maybe we should all dust off those things we've given up on. Maybe we should put on a new set of goggles and attempt to see the world the way God sees it, and not the way the world tells us to see it.

God's definition of success is much different than our definition of success.

These definitions aren't even in the same ballpark. They are polar opposites.

We look at numbers.
God looks at hearts.
And even one heart is just as important as 10,000.

"For all that is in the world, the lust of the flesh, and the lust of the eyes, and the pride of life, is not of the Father, but is of the world. And the world passeth away, and the lust thereof: but he that doeth the will of God abideth for ever." – I John 2:16-17

True Love

God loves us enough to discipline us.
God also loves us enough to die for us.

Those two motivations seem like polar opposites, but they really aren't. They arise from the same source: Love.

God's love is a double-edged sword; it is both righteous and forgiving. Grace and Holiness are married in a perfect union.

God's love perfectly balances both of these facets of perfect love.

Human love fails at balancing both of these aspects of love. Human love normally errs to one side or the other, and in many instances our actions may be proper but our motivation is misguided or selfish, thereby nullifying the power that perfect love has to offer.

If we desire to love with the same love God loves with, then we must strive to learn from God how to balance both of these perfectly. This process of learning shall never cease, for God's love is an infinite love that manages to balance each of these sides of love perfectly in an almost infinite number of unique circumstances.

Also, in each unique circumstance, the motivation is pure and based on love.

The only way we can love this perfectly is to be in constant communication with God, relying on his infinite wisdom and love to flow through us uniquely for each person and circumstance that is presented to us.

So, if we want to love the way God loves, our only choice is to get REALLY close to God.

The degree to which our love matches God's love is solely based on how close we are to God.

"We love because He first loved us." – I John 4:19

Prayer

What is Prayer?

Prayer is communication with the one who gave you the ability to communicate.

Prayer is sharing your heart with someone who formed your heart.

Prayer is telling someone your needs who already knows your needs before you tell them.

Prayer is asking forgiveness from someone who has already forgiven you.

Prayer is having a relationship with someone who made you for the express purpose of having a relationship with you.

Prayer is placing your knees on the earth to talk to someone who fills the highest heavens.

Prayer is asking for someone else's will to be done in your life who wants the best for you.

Prayer is having a one-on-one dialogue with someone is able to have an unlimited number of conversations simultaneously, but who cares for you as if you were the only person in the universe.

Prayer is revealing yourself to someone who already knows you better than you know yourself.

Prayer is a dialogue that doesn't leave you unchanged. Prayer literally transforms you.

Even though God knows all things about you before you even utter a sound, He still longs for you to just talk to Him.

He wants to talk to you with such intensity that He gave His one and only Son so that you could come to Him directly with every thought, emotion, fear, request, and praise.

You don't need to use fancy words, or religious jargon.

Open your heart to Him, and He'll open His heart to yours.

Don't let that incredible privilege go to waste. Don't let the busyness of this world distract you from the one thing that will give you the strength to make it through this world.

And don't miss out on the relationship of a lifetime.

"Rejoice always, pray continually, give thanks in all circumstances; for this is God's will for you in Christ Jesus." – I Thessalonians 5:16-18

Doubting Thomas

Logic and empirical evidence are not sufficient on their own to comprise true faith. Something else is needed.

If this is true, then why did Thomas only believe after he was able to see the scars on Jesus?

This type of evidence (the scars) "leads" us to the truth, but it's not the underlying reason "why" we believe. The why is outside of ourselves, and it's outside the realm of our objective experience. The "why" has more to do with our heart than it does any amount of evidence.

In my own personal journey, I've had all the evidence at my disposal, and still found myself disbelieving, and I've had virtually no evidence and found myself believing- yet, I have to admit that empirical data served a purpose to provide a path where I could be "exposed" to the truth. The evidence itself was not that truth, nor did it cause ultimate faith in that truth- but it did help to identify that truth. And after that identification is made, we are still asked to "believe" in the object of that truth. That's a separate process.

Thomas needed that path laid out for him to be led to the Truth, but it was ultimately that Truth that transformed his heart to believe, where Jesus became the source and reason of that belief. The evidence is never the source or the reason.

We know that there are a group of beings that have been provided with much more empirical evidence than we have ever been presented with, and yet they still do not "believe". What does it mean to say that the demons do not believe? I mean, do they really not believe in the sense that they would say, "God doesn't exist because I see no evidence of Him"? That would be like me showing you a book in my hand and you claiming that I don't have a book in my hand. No, the angels are all given the same amount of evidence of God's power and existence, and yet some do not believe and some do. But what kind of belief are we talking about?

Obviously, this definition of belief includes something much different than simply asserting that something exists. It has the connotation of following, trusting, and aligning your direction to be in agreement with the source of that Truth. That's something that no amount of evidence will command.

The person who has "seen and believed" is someone who had evidence, but they still needed an act of faith that brought them into alignment and trust in the source of that evidence. That's the act of faith that all people must go through, regardless of the amount of evidence they are given.

It's a quantum leap from simply being agreeable that the evidence being presented to you is true. It's that leap that the demons will not make, and they have all seen His scars, and much more than Thomas ever saw.

True belief cannot be conjured up with more evidence. This is why Jesus said that even if He were to die and come back from the grave, some would still not be able to believe. He was pointing out that it was not evidence that these people lacked. They lacked a heart that was in line with desiring to know and follow the Truth. The demons are not in want of more evidence.

Evidence can help lead someone whose heart is prepared to come to faith. But evidence is completely worthless to someone whose heart is not in the right state.

———————————————

"For we live by faith, not by sight." – 2 Corinthians 5:7

The Power of Perspective

Good stuff happens to bad people.
Bad stuff happens to good people.
Bad stuff happens to bad people.
Good stuff happens to good people.

If we make any of those four statements above, we must answer these questions:

How do you define "good stuff"?
How do you define "bad stuff"?
How do you define "good" people?
How do you define "bad" people?

I think you will find that it's difficult for us to define those terms, and everyone will have a different definition. And we'll find that God's definition for each of these terms is radically different than ours.

For example, persecution would normally be viewed as "bad stuff," but one could easily argue that persecution is good because of its effect on the person being persecuted. Their faith and reliance on God increases, as does their endurance and their appreciation for life. In this instance, someone could argue that the gain in intangibles far outweighs the loss of tangibles, and that this exchange is a net positive. And in some people's accounting system, these things are much more valuable than material possessions, or health. For others, tangibles take primacy.

You can see that our perspective changes how we measure circumstances. A great deal comes down to perspective. Really, it's the only thing that matters.

Good circumstances can be bad, and bad circumstances can be good- all depending on perspective. Perspective can invert our definitions.

If perspective is in the driver seat, then it makes sense that we should focus most of our life's energy on what's driving the shaping of our internal perspective. We shouldn't spend our time focusing on the outward, we should focus on the inward.

Contrary to our inclinations, we all have very little control of the outward. But we do have control of the inward, and the inward then changes how we perceive the outward.

When the inward changes, the outward changes.

So in a sense, we have the power to change the outward without actually lifting a finger to change the outward. That's powerful. Yet, we're all hopelessly spending our life's energy trying to shape our external circumstances to conform to our internal desires. The smarter thing to do is to change our internal desires.

.

How do you view God? How do you value your relationship to God? How do you value this material world and all it has to offer?

Your answers to those questions define your perspective. And your perspective defines how you view everything else.

I think this is what Jesus meant when He said that we could all tell a mountain to move and it would move. Jesus wasn't saying that the mountain (external) would move. He was saying that the shift of our internal perspective of the mountain would cause it to move in our internal world. And that's where we live.

If I were to give myself advice, I would tell myself to stop spending my life running the rat race to make the external things around me move into the position that I've dreamed up for them. Instead, I would tell myself to run the rat race of moving my internal perspective to come into alignment with God's, so that I can see the world through His eyes.

When we ask God to give us faith, to live in us, and to transform our mind, our internal perspective changes.

Radically.

When you put on these new glasses, you will see that the mountain has moved.

Nothing about the external world has changed.

Only our perspective has.

And that's all that really matters.

Death Before Life

God started with a dead seed—the earth.
It was formless and void.
His Living Spirit hovered over the dead waters.
Everything was dead.

Then, He started speaking life and life emerged from the dead ground.

Death came before life.

Why didn't God create everything in a state of life from the very beginning? Why start with death?

We see this pattern repeating, and so we're compelled to dig deeper and discover the lesson God wants to teach us through this example.

God brought forth a dead man out of the soil (Adam) and then breathed life into him. Again, we see the pattern that death comes before life.

Man died when he ate the seed which came forth from the earth (the fruit). This tree is the Tree of the Knowledge of Good and Evil, and its fruit brings forth death. But, there is a second tree— The Tree of Life.

The first tree is death.
The second tree is life.

And notice, man chooses death first. Death precedes life.

God then sends forth His law which brings forth death to a dead people who did not follow Him.

God then sends forth The Word made flesh (His Son), who was full of life.

Again, the first is dead, and the second is alive.

Now, the Seed (Jesus) was put to death, buried in the earth, and raised again to new life. Even Jesus, Himself, experienced this pattern of death before life.

Spiritually, He asks for each of us to become like a seed and bury ourselves in a second death. When we follow this same pattern, we will be made alive.

Those who are made alive are asked to take God's Living Word (The Seed), and sow it into the dead ground (mankind). Those who respond are raised from the ground in new life, like a tree bearing much fruit.

Unless we first become like a seed and enter the ground and die, we cannot live.

In the beginning, man ate from the first tree- The Tree of Death.
In the end, man will eat from the second tree-The Tree of Life.

Man must first live in a physical body that experiences death, before he can live in a second body that experiences immortal life.

The beginning of the story was death.
The end of the story is life.

It's the story that God's been telling since the world began.

The lesson God wants us to learn is this: To live, we must first die.

Have you died to yourself?

"Now if we have died with Christ, we believe that we shall also live with Him,..." - Romans 6:8

"Truly, truly, I say to you, unless a grain of wheat falls into the earth and dies, it remains alone; but if it dies, it bears much fruit." – John 12:24

The Perfect World

I'd venture to guess that any one of us, given the opportunity to be a "god," would have created the universe with success built in from day one.

Humans possess an insatiable desire for instant success and gratification. We all want our dreams to come to fruition, and our fantasy world would be absent of struggle and filled with pure ecstasy and happiness.

Given the option, we'd just as soon be living on a beautiful island in a mansion, and fulfilling every single one of our desires.

Everyone would love us, and we would "love" certain individuals out of convenience and an ulterior motive.

Why go down a path of struggling and pain if it were not necessary?

Now, imagine that you're god and that you possess an infinite amount of power. You have the power to create any fantasy world or worlds that your heart desires.

Just say it, and it will happen.

What would your world be like?

Would it look like the world we live in now?

Would it involve your creation enduring untold amounts of pain and suffering?

Would it involve yourself, the chief architect, entering into your creation to suffer rejection, humiliation, pain, torture, and death?

Imagine having all of the power in the universe, and then freely and willingly *choosing* to experience rejection, torture, and death.

Yet, this is exactly the path we find God choosing.

God chose the path of pain, rather than the path of ease and comfort. God chose the path of serving, rather than being served.

In God's fantasy world, there is much suffering before ecstasy is realized.

Suffering for us.
Suffering for Him.

At first, this seems counterintuitive to our fleshly mind. Our fantasy world would be antithetical to this world. Our fantasy world would follow the easy road and it would most assuredly revolve around us.

But, our framework of thinking is limited by the fact that we do not have infinite wisdom.

God does.

And in God's infinite wisdom, He saw the value in marching down a path of suffering before being rewarded with the ultimate prize.

He saw value in rejection before being accepted.
He saw value in death before life.
He saw value in serving before being served.
He saw value in being humbled before being lifted up.
He saw value in nails before crowns.
He saw value in tears and heartache before joy.
He saw value in faith in the unseen before clear vision.
He saw value in turmoil before peace.
He saw value in complete loss before being given the keys to the universe.

Given the option, God chose not to take the easy path.

If you are in a season of struggle, please consider that the One with infinite power at His disposal chose to struggle first. There is value in this path that we are on.

Our grandest vision of a fantasy world pales in comparison to the treasure that God is creating through His process.

There is a reason why He chose this path. Imagine how wonderful the prize must be if God allowed suffering in this world to make this prize possible. He wouldn't have allowed suffering if the prize wasn't worth it. Therefore, our suffering is evidence that something much greater awaits us that our imagination cannot fathom.

Let Him work. Be patient. There is a treasure at the end, and this treasure supersedes anything we could ever imagine.

The Real Miracle

Many of us wonder why God doesn't speak to us audibly, or why He doesn't perform visible miracles on a massive scale to prove His existence.

After thinking about this some, I believe that what He does is even more convincing than the type of miraculous tangible manifestations that we all desire. I think we're asking the wrong question.

You see, you or I can do any of these things.

We can produce sound.
We can transport a song across the globe in a fraction of a second.
We can move massive objects with invisible force fields such as magnetism.
We can manipulate DNA and create a new gene that would make a limb completely regenerate right before our eyes.
We can create illusions of light, sound, and motion in the form of holograms that could fool the masses.
We can create photorealistic 3D simulations using virtual reality to fool the senses.

Relatively speaking, manipulation of the physical world is simple, and not outside the realm of human capability. Our ability to control the physical world will only increase over time.

But what we can't do with any amount of technology or physical effort is speak directly and privately to someone's soul.

We can't guide or lead someone silently.

We can't remove the weight of guilt and shame.

We can't absolve someone's sin from the universal accounting system.

We can't transform the way someone looks at the world by snapping our fingers.

All of these things are out of the reach of human capability. They are off limits. Inaccessible. To accomplish any one of these invisible things would be considered a miracle by human standards. Humans have great control over matter, but not the immaterial.

So why do we ask God to prove He is real by asking Him to do things that we can already do; things that are already in our sphere of influence? Where's the logic in asking God to prove that He's not human or the product of human invention by doing something that humans can do?

We want God to show us that He transcends the physical by manipulating the physical?

Why don't we ascribe more value to the types of miracles that take place in a realm where humans are completely incapable of manipulating a single thing?

Miracles that are not visible and that are immaterial in nature are the proof required to demonstrate that God is not of this world.

Why don't we ask God to prove that He transcends the physical by doing things that transcend the physical? Why don't we ask God to show us that He's not human by being, well,... not human?

Jesus' greatest miracle was not walking on water, turning water into wine, or raising someone from the dead.

Jesus' greatest miracle was forgiving someone's sins.

There's no one else in the universe that can do that.

Let's not ask God to put on a light show. Let's ask God to do only what He can do.... change hearts.

Make Each Day Count

How do you know if you made each day count while you were living on this earth?

Ask yourself two questions before you go to sleep every single night.

Make it a habit.

Did I love God with all of my heart, mind, soul, and strength today?

And,

Did I love others today?

How or how not? Get specific.

Jesus taught us that these are the two greatest commandments.

Do a true assessment. Be brutally honest with yourself.

When you've identified specifics of how you've fallen short, then tell yourself two things:

Tomorrow, I will do X to love God more with all my heart, mind, soul, and strength.

And,

Tomorrow, I will do Y to love others more.

You don't really need to make a list of ten things, because you'll never do them. Even though there's probably hundreds of things to work on, just choose one for each of the two questions so that you can focus on that one thing throughout the next day.

When you wake up in the morning, remind yourself of these two items for the day. Then, make it a point to do them. Throughout the day, remind yourself of the two things. In each situation you find yourself that day, ask yourself how to apply those two things in that situation. Ask God to give you the power and diligence to achieve those two things.

Then, when you're going to sleep that night, ask yourself if you did those two things, and where you've fallen short.

Keep repeating this each and every day. Ask yourself the two questions.

We're not perfect, so we're never going to be able to answer those two questions with an unequivocal yes. We will always identify a shortcoming. And the point is not to beat ourselves up over the shortcoming; the point is to strive to do those two most important things better each day.

If you take care of those two things every day, you can leave this earth saying that you made each day count.

Make the best of the time God has granted you while on this earth.

The Good News

As a teenager, I gave my life to Jesus while I was sitting at a table in a pancake restaurant. A friend who had introduced me to the Bible asked me if I wanted to become a believer. I said yes. I prayed with him, and that started my journey with Christ.

I didn't feel fireworks or experience an instantaneous radical transformation, but I did feel like my life had changed at that moment. This marked the beginning of a lifelong transformation that slowly, but surely, changed everything about me. There has been many ups and downs, but even after more than 30 years, I am still being transformed for the better, and I imagine that I will be for a very long time.

So, I ask you the same question: have you given your life to Jesus? God intends for faith to take center stage:

> Hebrews 11:1,3,6 – "Now faith is confidence in what we hope for and assurance about what we do not see..... By faith we understand that the universe was formed at God's command, so that what is seen was not made out of what was visible..... And without faith it is impossible to please God, because anyone who comes to him must believe that he exists and that he rewards those who earnestly seek him."

Now, why should you give your life to Jesus? To understand this, it's first necessary to turn this question around and ask why Jesus first gave His life for you.

The word "sin" is certainly not in vogue these days. Most people would chalk up sin to an antiquated concept that has seen its day. But before we discount the reality and seriousness of sin, let me ask you a question: has there ever been a time in your life where you felt guilt or remorse for doing something that you knew was wrong? Have you ever hurt someone else? Have you ever been selfish? Have you ever looked out for yourself while someone else suffered? Have you ever lied? Have you ever been puffed up with pride and arrogance? Have you ever wasted the time, money, talents, and resources you have been given? Have you ever been unthankful? Have you lived your life without giving God a single thought or any of your time?

I have done ALL of these things, plus many more in good measure. In fact, my list for today isn't looking very good. All of the things I listed above are sin. They take us away from God. We ALL sin. We're all in the same boat, and nobody is better (or worse) than anyone else:

> *I John 1:8 - "If we claim to be without sin, we deceive ourselves and the truth is not in us."*
>
> *Romans 3:23 - "For all have sinned and fall short of the glory of God."*

But why do we sin? Our sin arises from what we are made of. We are made of human flesh, and we are told that our flesh doesn't have the capacity to refrain from sinning. Our flesh does not have the capacity to please God, because it is selfish. We inherited our sinful flesh from the first sinner, Adam:

196

Romans 5:12 - "Therefore, just as sin entered the world through one man, and death through sin, and in this way death came to all people, because all sinned—"

Galatians 5:17 - "For the flesh desires what is contrary to the Spirit, and the Spirit what is contrary to the flesh. They are in conflict with each other, so that you are not to do whatever you want."

Romans 7:18 – "For I know that good itself does not dwell in me, that is, in my sinful nature (my flesh). For I have the desire to do what is good, but I cannot carry it out."

So what? Afterall, everyone sins, right? No big deal. Well, there is a problem. There is a consequence to sin. The consequence is death:

Romans 6:23 – "For the wages of sin is death..."

Unfortunately, the result of sin is death. Eternal death. Our mortality can be directly blamed on our sinful nature. That's pretty bad news. It would seem that our situation is completely hopeless. It is impossible for us to live a life without sin, and as a result we are all destined to surely die. Before we give up hope, though, let's keep reading the rest of that last verse:

Romans 6:23 – "For the wages of sin is death, but the gift of God is eternal life in Christ Jesus our Lord."

Did you catch that? God provides us with eternal life, and this is a gift that comes directly from Jesus. God left His dwelling to wrap Himself in flesh, and to live on the earth as one of us:

> *John 1:14 - "The Word became flesh and made his dwelling among us. We have seen his glory, the glory of the one and only Son, who came from the Father, full of grace and truth."*

The fact that the Creator would take on the form of the creation was foretold hundreds of years before it took place:

> *Isaiah 9:6 – "For to us a child is born, to us a son is given, and the government will be on his shoulders. And he will be called Wonderful Counselor, Mighty God, Everlasting Father, Prince of Peace."*

But why did He come? What was His purpose and mission? Was it just to send us greetings and to teach us a few lessons about how to live our life? Well, His purpose in coming was also foretold hundreds of years beforehand:

> *Isaiah 53:4-7 – "Surely he hath borne our griefs, and carried our sorrows: yet we did esteem him stricken, smitten of God, and afflicted. But he was wounded for our transgressions, he was bruised for our iniquities: the chastisement of our peace was upon him; and with his stripes we are healed. All we like sheep have gone astray; we have turned every one to his own way; and the Lord hath laid on him the iniquity of us all. He was oppressed, and he*

> *was afflicted, yet he opened not his mouth: he is brought as a lamb to the slaughter, and as a sheep before her shearers is dumb, so he openeth not his mouth."*

These verses record a very sobering message: God took on the form of a human so that He could come to this earth, be rejected by His creation, and suffer and die to pay the penalty for our sin. This was all planned before God even created the universe. Not only did God create us; He also rescues us. Jesus had one mission from the Father, and that mission was to die to pay the price for the sins of all mankind:

> *Romans 5:8 – "But God demonstrates his own love for us in this: While we were still sinners, Christ died for us."*
>
> *I Peter 2:24 – "He himself bore our sins" in his body on the cross, so that we might die to sins and live for righteousness; "by his wounds you have been healed."*
>
> *I John 2:2 – "He is the atoning sacrifice for our sins, and not only for ours but also for the sins of the whole world."*

After Jesus died on the cross, he was placed in a tomb and a large stone was rolled in place to seal the entrance. Roman guards were positioned to at the entrance to protect His body from being stolen. Even with these safeguards in place, Christ arose from the dead and escaped the tomb.

> *Matthew 28:5-6 – "The angel said to the women, "Do not be afraid, for I know that you are looking for Jesus, who was crucified. He is not here; he has risen, just as he said. Come and see the place where he lay."*

> *I Corinthians 15:3-4 – "For what I received I passed on to you as of first importance: that Christ died for our sins according to the Scriptures, that he was buried, that he was raised on the third day according to the Scriptures."*

It's quite incredible to think that the Creator of humanity would choose to become one of His creation and to die in their place, even while His creation rejected Him. Instead of us experiencing death, Christ experienced death. Remember the truth that the consequence of sin is death? Instead of that death being passed on to us, it was passed on to Christ.

What do we need to do in order to receive this wonderful gift?

> *John 3:16 – "For God so loved the world that he gave his one and only Son, that whoever believes in him shall not perish but have eternal life."*
>
> *John 11:25-26 – "Jesus said to her, 'I am the resurrection and the life. The one who believes in me will live, even though they die; and whoever lives by believing in me will never die. Do you believe this?'"*
>
> *Mark 1:14-15 – "....Jesus went into Galilee, proclaiming the good news of God. 'The time has come,' he said. 'The kingdom of God has come near. Repent and believe the good news!'"*

The only thing you need to do is repent and believe the good news!

> *Romans 10:9 – "If you declare with your mouth, "Jesus is Lord," and believe in your heart that God raised him from the dead, you will be saved."*

Would you like to give your life to Jesus like I did that day while I was sitting in a pancake restaurant? I can personally attest from my experience over the last 30+ years that you will not regret making this decision. There are many decisions you might regret in your life, but this is not one of them. Knowing that your sins are forgiven sets you free to live the life God designed for you and to freely serve the Creator of the universe.

If you are inclined, this is a prayer that you can offer to God:

"God, thank you for creating me! I know that I sin, and I want to turn away from those sins and turn to you as my Lord and Savior. Thank you for your forgiveness. I believe that you sent Your one and only Son, Jesus, to come to this earth and die to pay the penalty for my sins. I also believe that He was risen from the dead, and that He offers me eternal life. I want to give my life to You, and I desire for You to take control of my life. I am Yours!"

If you said those words and meant them with your heart, or if you offered your own prayer to God, I would love to hear from you. Please let me know that you are a new believer, and I would love to encourage you on your new journey.

Please send me an email to: **DrDougCorrigan@gmail.com**

If you enjoyed this book, you may also enjoy another book that I've written titled, "The Author of Light." In this book, I demonstrate how God embedded His complete identity in the laws of nature. You can find this book on Amazon, or at www.ScienceWithDrDoug.com

I am also available for speaking engagements (face-to-face, or virtually online). If you would like me to speak to your group about this topic, please email me at:

DrDougCorrigan@gmail.com

Made in the USA
Columbia, SC
26 November 2021

49679119R00115